Nothing
is
Impossible

the story of Beatrix Potter

DOROTHY ALDIS

Nothing is Impossible

the story of Beatrix Potter

drawings by Richard Cuffari

ATHENEUM   1973   NEW YORK

dedicated to
CORNELIA ALDIS PORTER
GRAHAM ALDIS WESTPHAL
CARREY ALLEN WESTPHAL

Contents

Introduction

IT SEEMS TO ME NOW that I was born wanting to write this book. As a small girl, Peter Rabbit, Squirrel Nutkin, Jemima Puddleduck, Jeremy Fisher, and all the rest, were very special friends. First, the Beatrix Potter books were read to me. Later, as I began to read by myself, I read and re-read every Beatrix Potter book I could find. All her storybook characters were a great part of my growing up.

About the time I began writing books, it was very difficult to learn much about Miss Potter. Although her delightful stories actually became classics, long before she died, she did not wish to meet the public. She enjoyed foreign visitors, and particularly Americans. Many children's book specialists from the

United States visited England and arranged to meet her. However, from my own writing experience, I respected her wish and never had the privilege of meeting her personally. But, over the years, whenever I visited England, I always managed to do some research on Miss Potter and gradually, I began to know a good deal about her.

Beatrix Potter was born over a hundred years ago. On my trips to England, I visited museums, libraries, and other public places where she spent many hours in her own research. I walked along the streets where she walked and got to know areas of London that were part of her life. I visited the countryside where she summered and Hilltop Farm where she lived most happily. Bit by bit, I got to know her world and, bit by bit, I began to know the world she lived in.

When *The Art of Beatrix Potter* was published, and after Margaret Lane published her book, *The Tale of Beatrix Potter*, my old interest in my own manuscript returned. As I read those publications, I found I had been piecing Beatrix Potter's life together with considerable accuracy and it was the appearance of these books that convinced me to finish my manuscript. I enjoyed writing it and I hope you'll enjoy reading it.

The people who write books are often asked lots of questions. The question that I am most often asked about my writing is: "Is it a true story?" I can only say it is as true as I could make it. The characters and main incidents are factual. The conversations are what I imagined them to be, but I think they were pretty much like you'll read them in this book.

DOROTHY ALDIS

Lake Forest, Ill.

Nothing
is
Impossible

the story of Beatrix Potter

Locked Up Tight

NEARLY EVERYBODY REMEMBERS a little of what it was like to be five years old. Quite a few people even remember some things that happened when they were four, or three, or even two.

But most children, when they are five years old, can hardly wait to be six, seven, or eight. When they get to be twelve or thirteen, they long to be grown-up so they can boss themselves. They hurry away from childhood days and soon forget most things about them.

This is a story about a girl named Beatrix Potter who never forgot what it was like to be a child of four or five or six. Perhaps this was because she spent so much of her childhood alone. Until she was almost six, she had no brothers or sisters. She never went to school or had any playmates her own age. Her parents did not seem to be interested in her. At least, they hardly ever saw her. As she grew older, they never played with her. They never gave her parties. They never took her for drives with them in their carriage. They lived in one part of the house, and she lived in another.

Mr. and Mrs. Potter and Beatrix lived in London, about a hundred years ago, in a tall stone house that stood around a rectangle called Bolton Gardens. Their house was Number Two. Crowding around were a number of other houses facing the same garden, each with a coach house in back and cooks, butlers, parlor-maids, and housemaids inside. The cooks were cross, the butlers grand, the maids wore caps with streamers. The butlers polished the silver, set tables, and served meals. It was the parlormaid who served tea.

However, these were things Beatrix Potter rarely saw, because at Number Two Bolton Gardens she did most of her living in a third floor bedroom that had nursery bars at the windows. Like a prison.

Nevertheless, the bars didn't keep Beatrix from looking out and down in the street. There were plenty of things to see: well-groomed horses harnessed to shining carriages driven by wonderfully neat coach-men who quickly climbed from their high seats to help ladies and gentlemen in and out of their carriages. Nurses with ribboned caps walking out with babies in perambulators. Delivery boys bringing groceries to kitchen doors. The lamplighter making his rounds at sunset. Birds flying about in the treetops of Bolton Gardens.

From her barred windows she could also watch the trees, bushes, and flowers of Bolton Gardens as they changed with the seasons. In winter the flowers disappeared for many long months, and the gardens were dreary with rain.

When she was five years old Beatrix still hadn't learned to tell time. By the clock, that is. Just the same, she knew when it was ten-thirty every morning, because it was then that her father left for his club. She knew he was going to his club because her nurse McKenzie told her so. McKenzie didn't say what this club of his was. Beatrix imagined it to be a huge stick, much heavier and larger than the silver-topped walking cane that Mr. Potter always carried with him. What did he do with such a great big stick? Beatrix knew she would never dare to ask him, so she might never know.

Promptly at one o'clock every day McKenzie would summon her for lunch. This had been carried from the kitchen up the back stairs on a tray, and was pretty much the same every day: a veal cutlet, sometimes a vegetable, and always rice pudding. Beatrix ate it alone while McKenzie went down to the kitchen to eat with the other servants. There were eight of them, because the cook, butler, parlormaid, and housemaid each had an underservant to help. No, there were nine, for the coachman ate in the kitchen, too.

After she had finished lunch and played with her wooden doll Topsy for a while, Beatrix would go to look out the window again, so she could watch her mother climbing into the Potters' carriage with the coachman's help. For her daily drive, Mrs. Potter wore a trailing skirt and often a feather boa which blew in the breeze as lightly as thistledown. Then shortly after three, if it wasn't raining (which it often does in London), McKenzie would take Beatrix out for a walk. The starched white dress she had been buttoned into early that morning was still very clean. Her striped stockings were very straight. Her black boots were gleaming. She looked like a little girl just taken out of a box, shining and new.

One summer day, when it was not only not raining but sunshiny and blossomy outside, McKenzie and Beatrix took their usual walk, which was past the Kensington Museum of Natural Sciences. As they were turning the corner of Queen's Gate—a wide street with many large trees—Beatrix noticed a sparrow picking and pecking away under a clump of lavender flowers that looked like bells. Beatrix knew their queer name: foxgloves. Although McKenzie did not talk much, she sometimes told Beatrix the names of flowers, because they made her homesick for Scotland.

"Poppies," she would say. "My mother's were ever so much bigger." Or, "That's snapdragon." Or, "Tiger lilies, if you like them. In Scotland we used to call them weeds."

"Foxes never wear gloves," Beatrix said to McKenzie as they proceeded slowly up Queen's Gate. And then, perhaps because it was such a pretty day and the sun lay on her back like a warm and friendly hand, Beatrix did something unusual for her: she asked a question.

"Do they, McKenzie?"

And McKenzie, perhaps for the same reasons, did

something unusual for her. She laughed. No, not that she'd ever seen, McKenzie answered. But not that she'd been acquainted with very many foxes, either.

Beatrix said, "If I drew a picture of a fox wearing gloves, he would look like a fox and his gloves would look like gloves."

"Well, now, I shouldn't wonder. The pictures you copy from your picture books are very good indeed."

Suddenly Beatrix thought of something quite different.

"McKenzie, did you know I have a new cousin? Because I *have* a new cousin. Mr. Cox told me so this morning."

Mr. Cox was the Potters' butler. Although every bit as grand looking as other butlers, Mr. Cox had learned to smile. At least, he had learned to smile at Beatrix.

McKenzie sniffed. "I shall tell Mr. Cox it's more fitting for your parents to tell you such family news."

Another question popped out. "What's family news?"

"A new cousin is certainly family news. Even though you have so many of them."

"But I never see them, McKenzie. They don't live in London, they live in other places. Anyway, I never see anybody."

McKenzie said, Yes, she knew. "But perhaps when you grow older and they grow older. . . . Well, this new one's only a baby, of course."

"Oh." Trying to visualize a baby, Beatrix squeezed her eyes shut. Of course, on her walks with McKenzie, Beatrix had often seen perambulators wheeled by nurses, but even on a beautiful day when the pram tops were rolled back, she was not tall enough to see what was inside.

Suddenly McKenzie stopped. "Beatrix Potter, listen to me!" The five words came out of her like a small explosion. "How do you think you'd like having a baby around the Bolton Gardens house?"

Looking up into McKenzie's face, Beatrix was surprised to see it turning a bright pink.

"Well, really, I'd rather have a mouse around. A mouse that was mine," she added.

"And what would you do with your mouse?"

"Love it and feed it." Beatrix clasped her hands together, as if she could really feel the mouse.

"But you couldn't have a mouse in the house!" McKenzie was shocked. "I mean as a pet. Although goodness knows there are plenty in the kitchen."

"Oh. . . . Do you suppose I could get one from the kitchen?"

"Certainly not!" And McKenzie started to walk on again.

After this odd and, for them, extremely long conversation, they were on their way home. No one was having tea in the parlor, so Beatrix guessed her mother and father must be out paying calls. They did not meet Mr. Cox in the hall, a disappointment to Beatrix. She had been thinking of something she wanted to ask him—something that couldn't wait.

Up in her room she took off her coat and hung it up in a huge, dark cupboard. She felt around in the cupboard, looking for something, but it was hard to find anything in the dark, especially if you weren't sure it was there.

"Well, I'll just have to ask Mr. Cox for a box," Beatrix said to herself. "And then I'll ask him for a mouse!"

After this decision she played with Topsy, putting her to bed and getting her up again; showing her picture books and pretending to read aloud to her until McKenzie said supper would be up directly. "So come and wash your hands. I've already poured water in the washbowl."

Beatrix knew what her supper would be: two soft-boiled eggs, toast, and either strawberry or currant jam. She knew because that was what it always was. There was nothing that was not always the same at Number Two Bolton Gardens. Beatrix would have been astonished had she been told that before she got up enough courage to ask Mr. Cox for a box, a most extraordinary thing would have taken place at Number Two.

An Upsetting Morning

THE DAY BEGAN EARLIER than most days. And strangely, McKenzie said, as she was helping Beatrix dress,

"You're so grown-up now, I'm sure you'll be able to put on your own dress and button it and lace your own shoes. Right now I have to have a word with Cook."

McKenzie had never had a word with Cook before that Beatrix could remember. McKenzie and Cook didn't like one another. Anyway, why this minute, when she was standing waiting for her dress to be slipped over her head and her stockings pulled straight?

Still in that brightly cheerful manner McKenzie said, "Besides, your grandmother's here, and she'll be coming to see you any minute now."

So early in the morning! But her grandmother never came before teatime! While Beatrix waited for old Mrs. Potter to appear in her black dress and white cap trimmed with black ribbons, she managed to struggle into her dress. She gave up on the buttoning for the time being, and began lacing her shoes instead. Her head was bent over this complicated business when her grandmother's voice said,

"Here's Piglette. He may visit for a much longer time today."

Piglette was a stuffed pig made of white flannelette. Grandmother had brought him to visit once or twice before, and he and Topsy were friends. Surprisingly, Grandmother had told Beatrix that Piglette used to belong to Beatrix's father when he was little. It was impossible for Beatrix to imagine her stern, tall father with his dark side-whiskers as a little boy, but it was good to have Piglette in her arms again. Looking up to thank her grandmother, Beatrix was surprised to see that Mrs. Potter seemed worried. Thinking she knew why, Beatrix explained that McKenzie wasn't in the nursery because she had had to go below and have a word with Cook.

"Yes. Well, everybody's pretty busy this morning. Shall I help you with your shoes?"

"McKenzie says I'm old enough to lace them myself. After all, I'm five years old—almost six, really."

"I know. You'll be six in July, won't you? Perhaps too old to have a nurse?"

Beatrix stared at her grandmother. "Not too old to have McKenzie. I've *always* had McKenzie."

"I know. But when girls get to be five or six, they should learn to read. That's what books are for—to be read—not just to be looked at."

Both shoes were laced after a fashion now, and Beatrix reached for the pearl dress buttons beneath her chin. She managed to get the highest one done while she was thinking about what her grandmother had said.

"If I have to read, why can't McKenzie teach me?" she asked.

"Because nurses don't teach. Governesses do."

"What's a governess?"

"A lady who teaches. She teaches writing as well as reading. Languages, too."

Beatrix didn't bother to ask what languages were. "But why can't somebody teach McKenzie to teach, and then *she'd* be a governess?"

"Because McKenzie wants to keep on being a nurse. A nurse to somebody else. . . . Here, I'll finish those buttons for you."

Beatrix had forgotten all about the buttons. "A nurse for *somebody else!*" Even when she hurt herself badly Beatrix rarely cried, but right now she felt so confused that tears pricked her eyes. They didn't

run down her cheeks, though. Not that.

"A nurse for what?"

"For a baby, of course."

Beatrix couldn't believe her ears. "Whose baby?" she asked.

"Your mother's and father's. His name is Bertram. He was born at four o'clock this morning, and he weighs eight pounds. Isn't it wonderful?"

But Beatrix couldn't think about it's being wonderful.

"And McKenzie is going to be *his* nurse?"

"Yes, dear. Because now you are getting to be such a big girl you don't need her any longer. You'll have the governess instead."

"When will the governess come?" Beatrix was feeling a little frightened.

"Oh, dear, didn't anyone tell you? Tomorrow."

And sure enough, a Miss Duncan came early next morning, but she only stayed twenty-four hours. It wasn't because she didn't like Beatrix, she explained. What she didn't like were the rules for living at Number Two. She felt she shouldn't have to eat with the cook, butler, parlormaid, housemaid, and all their underservants. She felt she should be invited to eat with Mr. and Mrs. Potter. When it was suggested to Miss Duncan that she have her meals with Beatrix on the third floor, she said this was something she had never done: have any meal on any tray on any third floor.

Beatrix was glad to see Miss Duncan go.

Next came Miss Slaughter, who was older and grayer and had a bad knee. She felt the same way about the customs of Number Two, and she did not stay either.

So Beatrix was lucky twice. Besides, her grandmother stayed two whole weeks and often came to visit on the third floor. She helped Beatrix with her dressing when she needed help, but as a matter of fact, Beatrix was beginning to manage fairly well by herself.

One morning her father came to see her. Beatrix had hardly ever been alone with her father and she tried hard to think of something to say to him. But what?

However, this morning Mr. Potter smiled quite kindly. Noticing Piglette he said, "Why, if it isn't Piglette!"

"Yes," Beatrix said shyly. "Grandmother brought him."

"McKenzie is planning to show you your brother soon," Mr. Potter said next.

Beatrix couldn't imagine what to say to that, so she said nothing.

"You're going to like your brother," her father said. "And in a few days you may see your mother."

"Has my mother gone away someplace?" Beatrix asked, surprised. After all, if a brother could suddenly appear, governesses come and go, her father climb the steep stairs to see her in her third floor room, then anything could happen.

"Of course your mother hasn't gone away. She's resting in her room. Having a baby is tiring."

"Didn't she want him?" asked Beatrix.

"Of course she wanted him. Every mother wants a son. Every father does, too. But now it's time I started for my club. Be a good girl, Beatrix."

"Yes, Papa."

Immediately after lunch McKenzie appeared with a bundle in her arms. She was looking down at the bundle and smiling. "Here's your big sister, Bertram," she said to the bundle. "She's going to teach you lots of things. And like you very, very much."

The bundle screamed.

"Come look," said McKenzie, seating herself in a comfortable low chair. Beatrix approached with caution. That wrinkled, ugly, squirming thing a baby, a brother, a son that both her parents wanted, and she was supposed to *like*?

She turned her eyes away.

"Do you have to be with him all the time, McKenzie?" she asked in a voice so low it was almost a whisper.

"Not every minute, no. He's such a good baby, he sleeps a great deal, so I'll be able to slip up and see you."

"Often?"

"Fairly often. That is, until Miss Hammond comes."

"Miss Hammond?"

"Your new—that is, your next new governess. Your grandmother has interviewed her."

"What's interviewed?"

"Talked things over with her. Explained about eating in the nursery. Your grandmother feels certain she'll be a good teacher and that you'll like her very much."

All these people I'm supposed to like, thought Beatrix angrily.

"Oh, McKenzie, when is *she* coming?"

"Tomorrow."

for a second, giving her an encouraging pat on the
head. She isn't going to tell, thought Beatrix in relief,
and settled herself more comfortably to listen.

Now her father was opening the parlor door. "Good
afternoon, Mother, Helen won't be down for tea. She
is still feeling tired, you know."

Almost at once the parlormaid was bringing in the
tea tray and setting it down on the table. Beatrix could
imagine just how it looked—the heavy silver teapot,
the dainty cups and saucers, the plates of thin bread-
and-butter sandwiches, and other plates of cake or
cookies. If she had not been so excited she would have
felt hungry.

"Well, Rupert." It was her grandmother's voice
this time. "What do you think of your son? Flourish-
ing, isn't he?"

"Bertram has an unusually well-shaped head." Beatrix could hear the pride in her father's voice. "I think
it likely he'll be a most intelligent boy."

"And what will he do with his intelligence?" Her
grandmother's voice sounded almost sharp.

"What do you mean, do with his intelligence?"

"I was hoping he would use it more than you
have yours."

"Thank you, Agnes, we can manage nicely now,"
said Mr. Potter suddenly to the parlormaid, and Beatrix heard her close the door as she went out. Then
Mr. Potter spoke again.

"My dear mother, I'm afraid I don't know what you're trying to say."

"This. You do nothing with your life. Unless you consider reading papers at the Athenaeum Club, having lunch there, perhaps playing a game or two of whist before paying calls in the afternoon——. You spend your time killing time."

"Have you forgotten I'm a barrister?" asked Beatrix's father in astonishment.

"I've not forgotten you were trained to be one but you practiced law for exactly one month."

Beatrix couldn't imagine why her grandmother was speaking so strictly to her father—the way she sometimes spoke to Beatrix when she wasn't standing up her straightest or sat slouching in a chair. As she listened to her father—of all people—getting a scolding, she was slow to realize that a cooky was being secretly lowered to her. A ginger cooky, delicious, but so crisp she had to suck it before chewing in order not to make a crunching noise.

"I am also a photographer," said Beatrix's father, as though making excuses for himself.

"Indeed, you are not only a photographer, you are an excellent one. But how would you have been able to buy all that expensive equipment or live as you do with nine servants, if your hard-working ancestors hadn't left you a great deal of money?"

"Really, Mother, I could hardly help that," said Mr.

Potter, huffily.

"No. But far too many men these days consider it enough of an occupation simply to spend an inheritance, if they happen to have one. It also seems ridiculous to me that they feel it a disgrace to be in business. What's wrong, pray tell me, with being a banker? Or a publisher? Or running a store, for that matter? Your father was a businessman, Rupert. And so was your wife's father, for that matter."

"I know, I know."

"I imagine you would much rather have had him be a distinguished barrister and practice law. I know how that sounds. Blunt and disagreeable. I'm saying it because I've begun to worry terribly about your children."

"My children? My children will never lack for advantages!"

"Good clothes, you mean? Generous allowances? An excellent education—for Bertram, at least? . . . But Rupert, I want them to *live* life, not just be blotters and absorb it. I pray their days on this earth may be interesting—and creative. They should *do* something with their lives, not just exist!"

Beatrix had a feeling her father was about to defend his blotterlike days, but if he had such a notion it was quickly dispelled as his mother went on.

"And another thing, Rupert. I feel I should remind you that you are half a Crompton—and Cromptons have always been doers." Here Beatrix's grandmother nudged her under the table, meaning, Beatrix felt sure, *Now pay strict attention.*

Beatrix did. As her grandmother went on talking, she learned that Cromptons had been well-known Puritans, who refused to accept the religion of the time. But unlike a number of other prominent Puritans, they didn't sail away on the *Mayflower* to found a new country in America. No, indeed. They preferred to stay in England, to stick it out there.

"Your ancestors, Rupert, hoped to change England! Perhaps you remember what happened to some of them."

"Their arms and legs stretched wide in stocks; a painful procedure, I'm sure. Thrown into prison. Some even executed, perhaps."

"I do not think any were actually hanged," said old Mrs. Potter seriously. "But they would not have shrunk from even that. You remember the story about my own father—your grandfather, Rupert!—about how he visited a man in prison, who was accused of treason, even though he knew it would mean the loss of his own position as a judge? It wasn't sensible, it wasn't prudent. But oh, Rupert, can't you see how vigorous and *alive* they were?"

"A rather disturbing lot, it seems to me. Personally, I prefer a quiet existence."

"I know you do. But your children, I hope, will have the desire and opportunity to get something more out of life—even if it means facing difficulties. I want them to be prepared for it. More tea, Rupert?"

"Thank you, yes."

The sound of tea being poured, the clink of spoons against china. Now another cooky. In grasping it, Beatrix felt the reassuring pressure of her grandmother's hand. It seemed as though that warm old hand was saying: Be patient. Just keep on listening.

As she listened, Beatrix learned about a Samuel Crompton who had invented a new kind of spinning wheel in 1753. It was named The Mule because Samuel was so mule-like stubborn himself. People thought he was out of his mind not to settle down to being a prosperous farmer like his two brothers. But Samuel had stubbornly worked at his invention, and supported his wife and family somehow by playing the violin at the Bolton Theater. He had played at evening dances, too. He and his violin were in great demand, but then Samuel lost his right hand in a carriage accident and could no longer play the violin. An even greater blow was the fact that after the accident he didn't have the money to take out a patent for his spinning machine. He sold it for practically nothing, and it immediately became a great success. "Oh, well," Grandmother said, "a sad story, but just remember, while everyone thought he was attempting the impossible, he did invent that wheel. You'll find it described in every book about spinning and weaving. In fact, it is still used in remote parts of England. And then, of course, there was old Ab'ram."

Mr. Potter said rather crossly, "Haven't we heard enough about the Cromptons for a while?"

"Very well, I'll spare you Ab'ram. However, if you should ever care to learn about him, you can read of his accomplishments in history books. An eccentric man, yes. But in his own way he triumphed. . . . What I am trying to say, Rupert, is that all those Cromptons were men of character and conscience. *Workers,* Rupert, *workers.*"

Underneath the table, Beatrix nodded her head. She understood the point that was being made: that Rupert Potter was no worker and that it would be a very good idea if his daughter became one. But work at what? *She* couldn't invent a spinning wheel. She couldn't triumph at anything.

Nevertheless, an idea started spiraling upwards: If she was stubborn enough, if she turned into a true stubborn Crompton, might she just possibly not have to live forever behind bars at Number Two Bolton Gardens? It was an exciting idea.

Yet it was an idea that left Beatrix feeling torn, because even though she would love to accomplish something for her grandmother's sake, still she felt safe on that third floor behind those bars. Sometimes when she and McKenzie took their solemn walks together, Beatrix saw boys and girls playing in parks. Hiding behind trees. Running and screaming. Skipping ropes on sidewalks. What would they think of a girl who didn't know how to do any of these things?

That she was stupid?

Would they laugh at her?

More probably, they wouldn't notice her at all.

With these thoughts running through her mind,

Beatrix scarcely noticed when her grandmother and father left the parlor and she was free to leave her hiding place. It wasn't until she was up in her room again that Beatrix remembered she still hadn't learned about old Ab'ram Crompton.

Why Are You
So Frightened?

A FEW DAYS AFTER THAT never-to-be-forgotten adventure under the tea table, Beatrix heard a knock at her door. It couldn't be McKenzie, she thought, and it couldn't be her grandmother—they wouldn't have knocked. And, thank goodness, it couldn't be her father, either. She had watched him, beard, silver-topped cane and all, from her barred window as he walked toward his club. A club she was able to name now: The Athenaeum.

There was a second knock.

Could it be Miss Hammond? Beatrix froze with terror as she saw the door being slowly opened, first a crack, then a very much wider crack. And then, wonder of wonders, Mr. Cox's head appeared, followed by Mr. Cox carrying a box.

"May we come in?" he asked, walking into the room.

Noises came from the box—scrabble, scrabble, scrabble. Gently Mr. Cox set it down on the table where Beatrix ate her meals. The box had a door. Above the door Mr. Cox had painted three little windows. And above the windows there was a roof with a crooked little chimney, looking as if it might come sliding off.

Scrabble, scrabble again—and there was Hunca Munca sitting in her own doorway. She had the brightest and most noticing eyes. She had beautiful whiskers. Her long gray tail looped around and hung out the door of her house. No need to write "Hunca Munca Lives Here" when there was Hunca Munca herself, living and breathing, as anyone could see, and badly wanting to come out and explore this brand new world—brand new to Hunca Munca, at least.

"Will she like me?" Beatrix asked anxiously, hovering over the box, not quite daring to touch it.

"Bound to," said Mr. Cox. "Here." And from his pocket he produced a hunk of cheese wrapped in brown paper. "Break it up in small pieces," he said. "Don't try to feed her by hand at first. Scatter the pieces about the room. Let her get used to everything slowly. Well, now, I'd better go before McKenzie or your grandmother . . ."

"Oh, Mr. Cox!"

"What's the trouble?"

"I didn't hear you coming up the stairs."

"Well, you've been so busy admiring Hunca Munca I guess you didn't notice my feet. No shoes. See? And I tiptoed."

Beatrix sighed with relief. Certainly neither McKenzie nor her grandmother would ever think of taking off her shoes, let alone tiptoeing.

All that day she felt safe and happy as she played with her new friend. The next afternoon her grandmother came upstairs, but Beatrix heard her and had plenty of time to whisk Hunca Munca back in her house and put it away in the cupboard.

Beatrix's grandmother had a letter in her hand—a letter from Miss Hammond. Her measles had turned out to be German measles, which didn't last nearly as long as the regular kind. She was delighted to say she would be able to start being Beatrix's governess the following Monday.

"Now why are you looking so frightened?" asked Beatrix's grandmother after she had given Beatrix this news. "You must learn to read and write. It's necessary to learn a great many things in order to get along in this world. Besides, you are going to like Miss Hammond!"

"I want things to stay the way they are!" protested Beatrix.

Inside the cupboard she could hear an impatient scrabbling going on. By now Hunca Munca was accustomed to having the run of the room, of the whole third floor, in fact. She had become tame enough to eat tidbits out of Beatrix's hand; not just the cheese Mr. Cox had supplied, but nibbles from Beatrix's own meals. She even liked rice pudding. Listening to Hunca's demands to be released, Beatrix felt relieved that her grandmother was somewhat deaf.

"My dear granddaughter," old Mrs. Potter continued sternly. "We would all stagnate, we'd *rot*, if things remained always the same. 'The old order changeth, yielding place to new.' A poet named Tennyson wrote those lines. Every day of your life you're a whole day older, and even that's a change. You'll probably grow to be as old as I am. Possibly older."

Walking *slowly*? Bent *over*? Always wearing a white cap with black ribbons? Beatrix couldn't imagine such a thing. But neither her grandmother nor Tennyson, whoever he might be, had to tell her life was going to change. Wasn't Miss Hammond coming next Monday? Wouldn't Miss Hammond hate Hunca Munca? Mightn't Miss Hammond banish her? If only she, Beatrix, could be left quietly alone with her dear mouse, and with Topsy and Piglette, and of course her picture books.

However, at least one good thing began happening

again: afternoon walks with McKenzie. Although they couldn't exactly be called fun, still Beatrix was used to them, and it was comforting to be doing something familiar. It seemed that Bertram was such a good baby, (which McKenzie had not expected), he not only gladly ate, but gladly slept at all the right hours. So the housemaid had been persuaded to sit in Bertram's room while he napped and McKenzie took Beatrix walking.

On their walk up Queen's Gate on Sunday, Beatrix said to McKenzie, "Miss Hammond couldn't come when she planned because she was sick. If I were sick, would Miss Hammond have to stay away?"

"No, she could help take care of you. Come, don't dawdle. Bertram might wake up any minute now."

All day Sunday Beatrix worried about what she would do when Miss Hammond came. The only plan she thought of that was at all practical was to refuse to learn. She wouldn't need a governess if she wasn't learning anything. So tomorrow she would have to start refusing.

That night she slept with Topsy and Piglette on either side of her, and Hunca, in Hunca's house, at her feet. When she finally slept, that is. It took a long time.

She was still eating her breakfast on Monday when she heard feet coming up the stairs. Not walking. Running. It couldn't be her mother, father, grandmother, or McKenzie. No, nor Mr. Cox; butlers don't run. Beatrix dashed to put Hunca inside her house. This much she managed, but before she could get Hunca's house inside the cupboard, a voice called out,

"Is it all right if I come in? Oh, sorry if I'm disturbing you. I thought you must be someplace else since you didn't answer. . . . Why, how nice it is up here! In the treetops, really, and so sunny."

Bent over Hunca's house, trying to conceal it, Beatrix found she had no voice.

"I'm Miss Hammond. You must be Beatrix," the voice went on. "What have you there?"

The voice was young and friendly, but Beatrix still could not manage a single word. Nor did she look at the small figure that was suddenly kneeling beside her.

"But what a wonderful little house! Who lives in it?"

"Hunca Munca," said Beatrix through stiff lips.

"Who's she? Or he, if it's a he?"

"My mouse is a girl."

"Now this is truly making me feel at home. When I was a little older than you, I had three white mice, all girls. I taught them tricks. I had a rabbit, too."

In spite of herself, Beatrix was becoming interested.

"What was your rabbit's name?"

"Peter—Peter Rabbit."

Now Beatrix made herself look. Was Miss Hammond fooling her with all this talk about pets in order to somehow get rid of Hunca? But one look was enough to put such thoughts out of her mind. Miss Hammond's face was kind, her eyes brown and smiling. Her hair was black and glossy. Beatrix loved the striped muslin dress she was wearing.

Almost immediately things began to change at Number Two. Miss Hammond moved the furniture around in Beatrix's room so that it seemed a cozier place. One morning, she pushed the table where she and Beatrix ate their meals close to one of the big south windows. When the window was open, they could hear trees rustling. Birds looked in on them as they ate. One small gray bird with a yellow breast even perched on one of the window bars. Beatrix put a crumb on the bar for him, but he flew away.

It was a week before Miss Hammond said the word *schoolroom*.

"Let's fix it up the way we like it there, too," she said. "And by the way, if you think Hunca Munca isn't going to be with us while you're learning to read, you're wrong. Who wants an ignorant mouse around?"

Miss Hammond spread out Beatrix's books on a table in the schoolroom. She was interested in the pictures Beatrix had copied of animals and left inside the books.

"These are good," she said. "We must find some live models for you."

"What are models?"

"A real flower, if you are drawing it. A real animal, if you are drawing it. Or a real person, of course."

"I don't want to draw people. But could I draw a picture of Hunca?"

"That's what I hoped you'd say."

In no time at all Mr. Cox, Miss Hammond, and Beatrix solved the problem of any small traces Hunca might leave. Every morning Mr. Cox appeared with a bag which he held open for the depositing of Hunca's traces, always neatly wrapped in paper.

"Good morning, Miss Hammond. Good morning, Miss Beatrix."

"Good morning, Mr. Cox. Look at Hunca. She's learning to climb up my leg."

"A remarkable mouse."

Now instead of crawling, Beatrix's days began to run. Reading and writing, the way Miss Hammond taught them, were fun. She had a way of making unexpected jokes that kept Beatrix giggling, but they fixed things in her mind, too. She had forgotten all about refusing to learn. Now she wanted to learn as quickly as possible, and she was soon spelling her way through the storybooks where she had only looked at the pictures before. Writing came easily, for Beatrix could copy shapes of letters as quickly as she copied leaves and flowers.

But her days were not all study. She and Miss Hammond took all kinds of walks. They explored new streets. In a pretty little park, Miss Hammond dis-

covered mushrooms growing in a circle. She said she
was sure the Irish were the first to call this circling of
mushrooms Fairy Rings.

"Why?" Beatrix asked.

"Because Irish people believe in fairies more than
any other people."

"Why?"

"They just do. Now, how would you spell mushroom? Take the first part—*mush.* . . ?"

"M-u-c-h?"

"Well, no, that's not quite right. Spell it m-u-s-h.
You'd spell the mush you sometimes eat for breakfast
the same way. Only you must never eat mushrooms;
except for the ones you buy from the market."

"Why?" Beatrix seemed to love the word.

"Because some of them are poisonous. You might
die from eating just one bad mushroom."

Beatrix looked thoughtful. "But couldn't I use
them for models and draw them?"

"An excellent idea. We'll bring paper and pencils
tomorrow. Now, would you mind if I asked you to
spell *room*?"

"R-u—" began Beatrix, and was quickly corrected.

"Good. Now I'll stop pestering you except to ask
where you're going when we get home."

Beatrix obliged. "Straight up to my r-o-o-m."

"Good girl. You really are learning."

Beatrix gave a skip at the thought of learning.

Already Beatrix had been practicing her drawing with a number of models. Hunca Munca was the first, of course. Hunca certainly didn't sit still for very long at a time, but occasionally she would be tired enough to rest. One day Beatrix drew a bonnet on her, set way back so as not to be uncomfortable for her ears. This gave Beatrix an idea. Why mightn't Hunca be a lady, even a mother? Why couldn't they find a husband to live in that little house with her?

Mr. Cox did just that. He found Appley Dappley. The two mice got along very well together. Miss Hammond and Beatrix waited for them to have a family.

Miss Hammond had other ideas for models, too. She sliced oranges in half for Beatrix to draw. She encouraged Beatrix to bring home flowers from their walks—foxgloves, canterbury bells, even bramble leaves and mushrooms. Then there was the kitten who lived next door and who sometimes squeezed its way through the iron fence that divided the two properties.

"What shall we name her?" Beatrix asked.

"How about Tom Kitten?"

"But we're not sure it's a he."

Well, Miss Hammond said, she was sure; this was such a very bold kitten.

One day Miss Hammond surprised and delighted Beatrix by giving her a paintbox. Now she could draw in colors!

The first thing she tried to paint was a butterfly, but what a terrible model it turned out to be. Never still for one second, always fluttering toward some delicious blossom. Miss Hammond said not to worry, they could go to Kensington Museum, and there Beatrix could paint the butterflies they kept behind glass.

"Not living, of course, but painlessly killed. And don't I remember your saying you'd like to draw squirrels, if they weren't always climbing and racing around? Well, there'll be squirrels in the Museum, too. There are all sorts of animals, doing many of the things they do outdoors. It's a fine way to study them."

"But how can they keep the animals like that? I thought dead animals had to be buried."

With one finger Miss Hammond tilted Beatrix's pointed chin.

"When animals are needed for museums or collections, their insides are removed—stomachs, hearts, lungs, and everything else. Then the skins are tightly stretched around clay models of the animals and sewed up. Result—you have a model of the animal that looks almost exactly as if it were alive. Taxidermy is the word for this process."

Beatrix looked thoughtful. "Do you think I could do such a thing?"

"If you wanted to, I suppose. But I can't imagine its being a very pleasant occupation. And I suspect your parents would not be very happy if you turned into a taxidermist."

To this Beatrix agreed. "But my grandmother wants me to be stubborn. She wants me to work hard and *do* things. Well, perhaps I can think of something else."

When they were on their walks, they very often held hands, although there were plenty of moments when Beatrix broke away because she had just seen something she wanted to show Miss Hammond. It had never been any fun to show things to McKenzie.

Country Holidays

ONE AFTERNOON MCKENZIE brought Bertram up to the third floor. McKenzie had never said anything about the changes up there, and Beatrix thought she didn't even notice them. When McKenzie was with Bertram, Bertram was all she noticed. Bending over him now in an adoring fashion, McKenzie said she had news for Beatrix and Miss Hammond.

What now, Beatrix wondered. Another new brother? Someone has found out about Hunca? She had already lost Piglette, for her grandmother had thought it was time to take Piglette back to her own house for one of his long rests in the special bureau drawer.

McKenzie said, "Next summer, when Bertram is old enough to travel, we'll be going to Scotland for three whole months!"

"Why?"

"London's too hot for babies in the summer. They need a change of air."

"Well, I don't need a change of air," said Beatrix, wanting things to stay the way they were. Right now especially.

"Whether you do or don't, the whole household will be going, and you can't be left here all alone."

"All alone? But I have Miss Hammond!" Beatrix tried to explain, but McKenzie wasn't paying any attention.

Weeks flew by. The winter months passed, and as spring began edging into summer, Beatrix was unhappy. She knew Miss Hammond received letters that made her sad when she read them. Letters from her mother who was sick. Beatrix knew Miss Hammond had promised to spend the summer with her mother in Liverpool. When Mr. and Mrs. Potter and all their servants and underservants began planning for the trip to Scotland, all Beatrix could think of was that for three long months she wouldn't see Miss Hammond.

By now Bertram lived on the third floor with McKenzie. He had learned to crawl, humping up his fat bottom like an inchworm as he pushed forward. He adventured into Beatrix's room where he chewed her stockings, mittens, bedroom slippers, like a little puppy. He got hold of a portrait of Hunca Munca which he found delicious. Miss Hammond, Beatrix, and even McKenzie, who thought everything he did was perfect, tried to curb Bertram but this was difficult—he was so quick and so smart. Miss Hammond said he was an exceptionally bright little boy and would soon be a companion to Beatrix.

"What's a companion?"

"A friend, a helper. A person you'll like to have around."

At that moment, it was difficult for Beatrix to imagine wanting to have Bertram around all the time, but the very next day she was grateful to him. Hunca Munca gave birth to six babies on the folded quilt at the foot of Bertram's crib. Alerted by his shrieks, Beatrix found her brother staring at the babies with awe and delight—not touching, not pouncing, not doing anything he shouldn't do! With Miss Hammond's help, Beatrix moved the babies into Hunca's box, having first padded it with shredded paper—a family, a squirming, blind, hungry little family. Hunca looked proud.

"Do you know something I've noticed?" Miss Hammond said one day. "Bertram likes the same things you do: animals, flowers, birds. He tried to catch Tom Kitten yesterday. What a determined little boy he is!"

Beatrix explained that Bertram, besides being a Potter, was a Crompton. She told Miss Hammond about those stubborn early Puritan Cromptons, especially Samuel and his spinning wheel.

"Well," said Miss Hammond, "you and Bertram might do something remarkable someday too, you know."

"But what, for instance?"

"You never can tell." Miss Hammond hugged Beatrix cheerfully. "Just remember, nothing's impossible in this world."

"You sound like my grandmother," Beatrix said and then wailed, "Oh, Miss Hammond, when will you be going to Liverpool?"

"Not until you leave for Scotland, which is two weeks from tomorrow. And listen, when you write to me I want your letters to be neat and accurately spelled. Will you do this for me?"

Beatrix said, "There isn't anything I wouldn't do for you."

Miss Hammond said fine, because there were a number of other things she wanted Beatrix to do for her when she got back from Scotland.

"And you get back from Liverpool. I can hardly wait."

Miss Hammond laughed.

"That's another thing you'll have to learn to do."

"What?"

"Wait."

McKenzie turned out to be right about Scotland. The rented house was very different from Number Two Bolton Gardens, and much, much larger. It was called Dalguise House. Green lawns swirled around it, bordered by rainbow-colored gardens. To Beatrix it was full of enchantment. Standing quite still in the soft gray twilight, she could almost see the "little people" dancing in their fairy rings, or the beruffled and beribboned ladies and gentlemen who had once lived there.

Beatrix missed Miss Hammond terribly at first, but soon an unusual and comfortable thing happened: Mr. Cox began taking Beatrix and Bertram for long walks. This they couldn't possibly have managed if McKenzie, with so many of her family nearby, wasn't often gossiping with this or that relative, sometimes in the morning, sometimes during teatime. And twice McKenzie got permission from Mrs. Potter to drive over and visit two of her sisters who lived in a village several miles away. Of all odd sights! There went McKenzie, in a rented carriage, pulled by a not very well groomed horse, with the Potters' own coachman sitting grandly, high up in his seat, just behind the horses.

On their country walks Bertram, now a year old,

chattered in a language all his own, except that sometimes real words came out too. "Carrot," was one, for
he loved eating raw carrots; or "out," when he wanted
to get out of his pram.

Every once in a while, Mr. Cox would release him
for a short, ecstatic stagger. Then Bertram would
pounce on flowers, weeds, pine cones, sticks. One day
it was mushrooms. Instantly Beatrix snatched them
out of his hands.

"Poison, Bertram. BAD BOY. Poison."

"He's got so much to learn," she told Mr. Cox.
"As soon as he can understand anything, I'm going to
teach him everything Miss Hammond has taught me."

On their walks, Beatrix, Bertram, and Mr. Cox sometimes passed whitewashed cottages with vines clambering over them. Or farmyards with pigs, horses, and lambs. And hens, worried about their baby chicks, cluck-clucking to make them hurry across the dusty road. Living on a farm would be fun, thought Beatrix. So many things to see and do! Not at all like Number Two Bolton Gardens.

Bertram was good at making noises. He clucked like chickens. He grunted like pigs. Neighed like a horse. Baa-ed like lambs. In deeper country, the three explorers saw wild ducks swimming in a pond, minnows and water bugs in splashy streams. A frog sunning himself on a rock. A tidy mouse washing his whiskers under a big plantain leaf. As soon as they got home, Beatrix hurried upstairs to draw pictures of hens, sheep, a duck, a frog. With all her heart she wished Miss Hammond was around to suggest names for her new acquaintances. Puddleduck for a duck, perhaps? Fisher for that frog? Beatrix had seen him diving. Did he eat minnows?

Another good thing that happened was Mr. Cox's suggestion that she learn to press flowers and leaves on blotting paper. Bertram, standing on tiptoe and holding onto the table, watched with interest. Beatrix said to Mr. Cox:

"Miss Hammond will be happy to see these, won't she?"

"Indeed, yes," said Mr. Cox. "Why don't you write her about them?"

"I will. How do you spell press?"

"Two s's at the end."

"Like dress?" asked Beatrix.

"You're right. And while you're about it, why don't you tell her what a clever young gentleman your brother has become?"

"She knows that," said Beatrix, giving Bertram a pat on the head.

One day she told Mr. Cox she had found a dead bird. A thrush, she thought. And would Mr. Cox please help her skin and stuff it with leaves or grass? "I'd love to have him look alive just a little while longer."

Mr. Cox, who always wore his striped butler's trousers on these walks, said it might be even better to dig a grave for the bird, covering it with good black earth and planting a garden on top. This they could take care of all summer, weeding and watering it.

Beatrix thought this was a good enough idea, but not as practical as her own: burying a bird wouldn't teach her nearly as much as skinning and stuffing him. But she agreed to the burying when it turned out that Mr. Cox didn't know how to make a stuffed bird.

With so many fascinating things to do, the summer flashed by. Soon it was September. Next week they would all be going back to Number Two, where

Miss Hammond would be waiting for them.

But when they did return to Bolton Gardens, instead of Miss Hammond there was a letter.

Beatrix opened it with unsteady fingers. In Miss Hammond's neat up-and-down writing the letter said Miss Hammond's mother was worse and the doctor had decided she could not be left with just one old servant to look after her. The letter went on:

Beatrix, I know how sad you're going to be about my having to stay in Liverpool. I'm sad, too. But this is the way things are right now. So be a brave girl and a smart girl. Somehow, get yourself over to the Kensington Museum, as often as possible. I've written Miss Woodward to expect you. I'm about to write to your parents too, and McKenzie. There is no reason why McKenzie can't trundle Bertram over to the Museum. She can drop you off there and then take Bertram on to Stanhope Park, where he'll love exploring. Then they can pick you up in time for lunch. Of course, you are seven years old now and ought to be allowed to take that short walk by yourself. I'd write and suggest this to your parents, if I thought it would do any good. But just getting there is what's important, because you've already learned to teach yourself. My grandfather learned to read by the time he was three by pushing blocks around with big letters printed on them. Miss Woodward would love to help you with geography. Observe! Listen! And please practice writing as well as drawing. I don't want to hurt your feelings, but your handwriting could be a little bit easier to read.

Listen, good girl, ask Miss Woodward about words you don't know how to spell. Ask Mr. Cox. Oh, dear, I'm afraid this sounds like a preachy letter, but one more thing I must say that you're not likely to believe: as a person grows older, the years go by faster. In no time at all you'll be a girl of eight. Then nine. Soon you'll be in your teens, thirteen, then fourteen, and on and on. If you talked to your grandmother about this, she'd say one spring bumped into another. Well, anyway, I love and miss you, Beatrix Potter.

After reading this letter Beatrix felt like crying, but naturally she didn't. After all, she was seven years old.

A Peculiar Winter

THAT WINTER AT NUMBER TWO Bolton Gardens was most peculiar. Bertram was going on two years old and Beatrix was seven. McKenzie was homesick for Scotland and her relatives, and talked about this a good deal of the time. She could hardly wait for next summer when they would all be going back to Scotland again.

But there was one pleasant thing that developed about McKenzie: she had begun to accept the mouse family! This was because Bertram loved the mouse family so much. He even talked Mouse Language to them. At least, this is what Beatrix told McKenzie he was talking.

"Quite unnecessary," McKenzie sniffed. "You know

very well your brother can say a great many words in regular human language. He's a remarkable child for his age."

"Oh, I know," said Beatrix. "He has learned to find my paintbox even though I hide it in a different place every day. He has learned to get the brush wet in a water pitcher. He has learned to *paint*." Beatrix's eyes twinkled mischievously. "He painted the streamers on one of your caps the other day—red and blue. I heard you grumbling because you couldn't find it. Come— I'll show you."

But even this wild sight did not annoy McKenzie. What *did* upset her was talk that the Potter family might possibly be spending their vacations in the English Lake District instead of Scotland. Beatrix heard her father discussing this with McKenzie. In the nursery, of all places, where he had not come for a long time.

Beatrix did not hear the beginning of the conversation between McKenzie and her father—she had been looking over her collection of pressed leaves and flowers—but she began listening when McKenzie raised her voice:

"Why, Mr. Potter, that Lake District is ever so much damper than Scotland. Rain. Rain. Rain. Of course Bertram caught a cold or two in Scotland, but I cured them instantly with honey and camomile tea."

"Oh, I know, I know," said Mr. Potter. "But with

Bertram going away to school when he's eight, we must begin building up his constitution."

"But to try to build up his constitution in the LAKE District," wailed McKenzie.

"Don't worry, McKenzie," said Mr. Potter. "We will be going to Scotland this summer. I've a lease for Dalguise House, you know. But I've heard of a castle which I may be able to rent in Wray, near Lake Windermere. In a few years, that is."

"In WRAY! That miserable damp town, with not one sprig of heather growing anywhere around! I have a brother-in-law who was raised there. I know the country well."

"Is he married to one of your sisters you used to visit in Scotland?"

"Yes, and believe me, sir, my sister would never dream of living in Wray."

"Well, a number of people do, you know," said Mr. Potter. "Come, come, McKenzie, don't fret. Undoubtedly Scotland next summer. But I thought I had better prepare you for the future."

"Yes, Mr. Potter," said McKenzie, meekly. Meekly for McKenzie, that is.

❧

Another nice thing about that winter was that no new governess was hired to take Miss Hammond's place. Beatrix wondered about that a little, but she didn't say anything. Perhaps her mother and father had forgotten she was supposed to be learning lessons. Anyway, she tried to go on doing the things she thought Miss Hammond would want her to do. She practiced reading, and even spelling, shutting her eyes and trying to remember just how a word looked. She worked hard at writing and sketching, filling little notebooks with drawings of leaves and flowers, and of course Hunca Munca and her family. Arithmetic she gladly forgot, but she went almost every day to the Kensington Museum, for apparently Miss Hammond had convinced Mr. Potter this would be very educational. Sometimes McKenzie and Bertram walked there with her; sometimes one of the servants took her and called for her later.

Once, when Mrs. Potter had some early shopping to do, she drove Beatrix to the Museum. Mrs. Potter thoroughly disapproved of this queer museum life for her daughter. Other girls her age stayed home and were taught to sew and embroider. Young girls should learn such things. They ought to know how to play the piano and be able to sing a few songs. Later, when they were fourteen or fifteen, a dancing master would come to the house and teach them how to dance so they could later still go to chaperoned parties where *Boys* danced with them.

While all this was running through Mrs. Potter's

mind, she thought about all Beatrix's cousins who would soon be coming to London from their country homes to go to London parties. Mrs. Potter supposed she would really have to invite them for tea; that would only be civil! But then, she reflected, it might serve another purpose. When Beatrix met her cousins, they could tell her that going to parties was the right thing to do and—well—even enjoyable. Goodness, she shouldn't be so shy, Mrs. Potter thought, impatiently, forgetting that Beatrix had never had a chance to know boys and girls her own age.

Mrs. Potter had been very quiet while she was thinking all this. Beatrix was quiet too as they went jogging along toward the Museum, clip-clop, clip-clop.

"Beatrix," her mother asked abruptly. "What is the name of that lady at the Museum? Miss Hammond wrote me, but I've forgotten."

"Miss Woodward, Mama."

"And what does she teach you?"

"She doesn't really *teach*," said Beatrix slowly.

"What does she do, then?"

Beatrix, looking very small in her white piqué dress over which she wore a woolen, fur-trimmed jacket, looked soberly up at her mother.

"She praises me."

"*Praises* you? Whatever does she praise you for?"

"Because I draw animals very ac—" Beatrix paused, frowning over the long, unaccustomed word, but then

out it came—"very accurately, and have learned a great
deal about their insides."

"Their——"

"Where their bones and stomachs and hearts are.
Things like that."

Beatrix could see her mother was gazing at her with
absolute horror. She couldn't imagine why. What
could be more interesting than knowing about the
bodies of all the little creatures? But perhaps, Beatrix
thought to herself, her mother might rather hear about
flowers. So she began rattling off what she had learned
about stamens, pistils, pollen. And what happened to
pollen when it was blown by the wind from one blossom to another. . . .

As they drew up in front of the Kensington Museum, the coachman clambered down from his high
seat to open the door for Beatrix. For ME! Beatrix
thought, preparing to descend. Just as she thrust out
one foot, Mrs. Potter laid a hand upon her daughter's
arm. Looking stern and sure of herself, she said,

"Beatrix, I really do not think . . ."

Beatrix turned her head. "Think what, Mama?"

"That it's right for you to keep on talking to Miss
Woodward about such extraordinary matters!"

Beatrix, pulling away from the detaining hand,
stepped down on the sidewalk. Every drop of Crompton blood was boiling up within her as she said,

"Mama, I must."

Inside the museum, Beatrix hurried past the displays of birds and fish and animals to the fossil room. There was Miss Woodward, sitting at her desk. She looked up and smiled at Beatrix.

Miss Woodward was young—a mere girl, though she seemed grown-up to Beatrix. She walked with a sort of hop because she was lame, and she reminded Beatrix of a bony little wounded bird. But her lameness did not make her slow or heavy. In fact, there was a jaunty air about her limp, as though she were saying, "See how easy it is for me to get about! Want to race?"

Her straight brown hair was pulled back behind her tiny ears. Her cheeks were rosy; her eyes were gray. She had a warm and understanding smile.

Miss Woodward liked children. She liked showing children the way things work in this world.

Although Beatrix was not aware of it, Miss Woodward had practically been given a child by Miss Hammond. Not only to teach, but, as Miss Hammond put it, to save. When Miss Woodward woke up in the morning, the first thought that came into her mind was of Beatrix, with her white piqué dress and her zebra-striped stockings, and her serious, eager eyes.

The morning that Mrs. Potter brought Beatrix to the Museum, Miss Woodward had arranged to have a pair of snails for her. These were plant-eating snails, she explained, and could be kept in a geranium plant pot. The earth in the pot should be kept very moist

indeed, and any dead geranium leaves or petals should be plucked and placed on top of the earth to crumble and rot. Did Beatrix have a geranium pot?

"Yes, Miss Hammond gave me one. But, Miss Woodward, if these snails are plant-eaters, won't they hurt my geranium? I wouldn't want anything to happen to it."

Miss Woodward said tiny snail nibblings would not

be likely to be harmful. "And what's more, Beatrix, if you introduce a worm or two into the pot, they will positively be good for your geranium."

"Why?"

"Because worms crawling through the earth aerate it. The worms create tiny tunnels through which air seeps. This is good for all plants. These particular worms are earthworms, of course. Mr. Cox can dig for some in the garden."

"And I'll be able to watch them in my own room! Oh, thank you, Miss Woodward! . . . Do you know what I think I'll name them? Mr. and Mrs. Bill."

Beatrix and Bertram
Are Free

SPRING CAME AGAIN, and then one day something happened that made Beatrix feel as though she had been whirled back to a year ago. Again there were quick steps running up the stairs; again the quick rap on the door while Beatrix listened, scarcely believing her ears. Then the door opened, and a merry voice said,

"It's I, Beatrix. Are you surprised?"

"Miss Hammond!" Beatrix breathed.

Miss Hammond nodded briskly. "Yes, dear. My mother is better—oh, not really well, but good enough so I can leave her for a while. So I wrote your father, and he said I could come back. Isn't it wonderful?"

"Oh, yes, it is," said Beatrix. "Now everything will be just like it was before."

The weeks went spinning by, and soon it was time to think of vacations plans again. To McKenzie's delight, there was no more talk about Wray Castle. Mr. Potter had decided to spend the summers in Scotland until his lease for Dalguise House was up. Besides, extensive repairs had to be made in the castle before it would be ready to live in.

Once more Miss Hammond went away to Liverpool to spend the summer with her mother. But she promised to come back in the fall, so Beatrix felt quite comfortable and happy.

Coming back to Dalguise House was, to Beatrix, like returning to a well-loved home. Here she could escape from the rigid routine of Number Two Bolton Gardens into the freedom of the countryside. There were old friends to visit in the fields and streams and farms; new territories to explore. Those summers, she recalled later, were the happiest days of her childhood.

When they got to Scotland, Beatrix was astonished at her father's passion for fishing. Off he would go in his high rubber boots, an old cap pulled down over his eyes, a canvas bag containing fishing tackle, bait, and a luncheon sandwich swung over one shoulder. He wore a shabby raincoat and did not carry his silver-topped cane. The first time Beatrix saw him leaving for his favorite stream she thought: "Well! That cane was just for show."

Another surprising thing: Mr. Potter was a good

fisherman. At least, he brought back a great many fish. He was most particular about how they were prepared in the kitchen which, so Mr. Cox told Beatrix, was a great harassment to Cook, who was never very happy about anything anyway. Beatrix, however, benefited from her father's fishing in an odd way. She asked Mr. Cox to persuade Cook to save the delicate fish skeletons so she could string them together and make a skeleton collection. She already had a flower and leaf collection. When they returned to London she would, of course, show her new collection to Miss Hammond and Miss Woodward.

Would her grandmother be glad about her father's fishing? Beatrix wondered. Or would she feel this was just one more time-filling occupation? Somehow, this didn't seem to be the sort of thing a Crompton would call *work*.

As Bertram grew older, he became an eager companion for Beatrix's summer activities. Mr. Cox found an outbuilding, almost concealed with vines. He helped Beatrix and Bertram clean it out and they immediately named it "The Museum." Here they kept all their treasures—collections of beetles, toadstools, frogs, caterpillars, snake skins. Once they found a dead fox. They skinned it, boiled the flesh off the bones, and kept the skeleton. They made little drawing books and filled them with drawings of rabbits, cows, sheep, and plants.

Quite close to the Museum, Mr. Cox discovered some bats. Beatrix told Bertram some of the interesting things Miss Hammond had taught her about bats. How for millions and millions of years they had slept in caves and crevices during the day. At night, though, they were busy flying around in the air, eating thousands of insects: gnats, flies, and moths.

Of course, Beatrix and Bertram immediately wanted to keep bats as pets.

"You'll be kept very busy catching enough insects to keep two bats properly fed," cautioned Mr. Cox.

"Oh, I know," Beatrix said. "Unless we left them out at night. We could leave the museum door open and maybe they'd come back for their daytime sleep. And at home, we could keep them in that old parrot cage in the nursery, and—perhaps we could teach them to eat crumbs."

"You're getting to have quite a menagerie," said Mr. Cox.

Several years passed before the Potters finally went to Wray Castle, near Lake Windermere, for the summer holidays. It was a very different place from Dalguise House. The castle was turreted and huge and, as McKenzie had predicted, damp and cold, but Beatrix did not think any damper or colder than Scotland. Anyway, McKenzie wasn't in the castle to complain. McKenzie had decided to live out her days in Scotland. So Bertram had no nurse and Beatrix no governess, for Miss Hammond, as usual, was spending the summer with her mother.

Mr. and Mrs. Potter almost immediately found themselves suitably occupied. One of Beatrix's aunts, who lived nearby, introduced them to many new neighbors. The neighbors were friendly, immediately calling on the Potters and asking them for tea. And the Potters, who never entertained at Bolton Gardens, asked their new neighbors back. Beatrix decided her father liked showing off his castle. She herself enjoyed hearing the hum of conversation in the parlor on summer evenings. If "parlor" was what one called the largest and most important room in the castle. It was more like a ballroom, really.

Also, a number of men invited Mr. Potter to go fishing. The countryside was studded with bright blue lakes. Like jewels. The fishing was not as good as in Scotland, but Mr. Potter did not complain of this.

As for Mrs. Potter, ladies invited her to see the local sights. Quite a number of famous people lived in the Lake District, especially writers, and Mrs. Potter was driven past their homes and gardens. There was even one famous woman writer! The ladies liked to wonder about her. Did she live just like other people? Did she have talks with Cook about meals and see that the underservants didn't quarrel with one another?

On several occasions, Mrs. Potter invited neighbors for drives in her carriage. It was not crimson lined like the Potters' fine carriage in London, but it was still sufficiently impressive for people living in a castle.

With their parents busy almost every day, Beatrix and Bertram were free to go about their unusual interests as they had in Scotland. With Mr. Cox's willing help, of course. But then, suddenly, unexpectedly, an even greater helper appeared. Mr. Rawnsley, the Canon of Wray.

Canon Rawnsley was the vicar of the town of Wray, and because he and Mr. Potter became friends, he often visited at the castle. The Canon dressed in black clothes and a high collar. He was impressive and even a little frightening, until Beatrix and Bertram discovered how interested he was in the earth and everything that so eagerly pushed out of it: trees, flowers, vines, mushrooms, weeds.

He took Beatrix and Bertram for walks about the countryside, pointing out interesting plants with his cane.

"Look at these mushrooms," he said to Beatrix one day. "Did you ever see such delicate coloring? And did you know there are thousands of different kinds of

mushrooms?"

"Miss Hammond showed me some once, and I drew them," Beatrix remembered. "Aren't they poisonous?"

"Well, you don't have to eat them, do you? Just study them. Not many people know much about mushrooms."

Beatrix was examining the tiny plant. "I could

draw them, couldn't I? And keep a record of all the different kinds I find? And learn their real names——"

"A splendid idea," the Canon beamed at her. "I shall call you Miss Mycologist—that's a person who knows about mushrooms."

Beatrix was a little alarmed. "It'll take me a long time," she said a little doubtfully.

"Let's begin right now. During the summer you can make quite a collection. I'll help you."

But the Canon was even more interested in animals: in their feeding and living habits; their bones and muscles; their intelligence—what, with patience, they could be taught. In fact, he told Beatrix and Bertram, as a boy he had not only observed animals but had done a great deal of skinning and stuffing himself. "Anatomizing," he called it. No, he'd never learned to make clay models to mount the skins on, he admitted, answering a question of Beatrix's.

Beatrix said, "Bertram is an artist. Maybe he could make models for you."

Canon Rawnsley looked down at Bertram. "Could you?" he asked.

"I would need clay." Bertram squinted up at him. "I can get you clay."

"Then I could try," Bertram replied. "But what I really want to be is a painter—or a farmer."

The Best Time of All

THIS VACATION was the best one of all. It was wonderful to live in the castle with the enchanting countryside to explore. The area was hilly and woodsy, laced with streams and lakes rich in the creatures Beatrix and Bertram needed for their collections and experiments. They explored it thoroughly and found many animals. They visited at farmhouses, where the farmer's wife often invited them into the kitchen for a glass of milk and a bun. Beatrix gazed fascinated at the wide fireplaces with gleaming pots hung about, or the broad mantlepiece above with china dishes and ornaments.

Another thing that happened about this time was

71

that Beatrix started to keep a journal. It was Canon Rawnsley who gave her the idea. "It must be wonderful to write," she said to him one day, thinking of the verses he wrote so easily.

"Well, if you really want to write, why don't you start with a journal?" the Canon asked briskly, always eager to start something new.

"But what could I put in a journal? I don't do anything exciting."

"Why, everything that happens—the places you visit, people you talk to, stories you hear. It isn't so much what you write—it's doing it regularly that counts. And the more you write, the easier you'll find it. Do try it!"

With those bright, commanding eyes on her, Beatrix couldn't say no.

"Well—I will. Actually, I did start one, a year or two ago. But it wasn't very good."

"Never mind. You're older now. And I'm sure once you start, you will find plenty to write about."

Beatrix laughed. "But no one will read it but me. It will be a very secret journal."

But how could she be sure no one would read it? Then she remembered the secret code she had made up when she first started to keep a journal. Carefully she practiced using it until she could write with it as quickly and easily as with regular writing. Now she could write just what she thought, and no one could read it. She could even write when other people were in the room. Sitting in a corner of the parlor, she could listen to the conversations and write them in her secret language. She often wrote in her journal when her grandmother was visiting. It was comforting to have her grandmother's company, as she quietly embroidered initials on sheets or pillowcases, or darned socks, or knitted. Old Mrs. Potter never asked Beatrix what she was doing, sitting with her small neat head bent over her notebook. No doubt she knew that her granddaughter wanted this project to be a secret.

Beatrix had a good deal of time to write in her journal at Bolton Gardens for Bertram was away at school now, and Miss Hammond had left her too. "I've taught you all I can, my dear," she told Beatrix. "Perhaps your parents will want you to have special governesses now for French and German, and you really should have lessons in drawing, too. I'll speak to them about it."

Miss Hammond was as good as her word. Before she left, she took some of Beatrix's drawings to show Mr. Potter in his study. "See what a careful draughtsman she is, and how true to life she draws. She has a most observant eye and a feeling for delicate detail. Do you not think, Mr. Potter, that this talent deserves further training?"

"Hm-m-m. Most interesting. I will consider what you have said."

With this Miss Hammond had to be content. But after thinking it over, he did arrange for a Miss Cameron to give Beatrix drawing lessons from time to time.

No new governess threatened after Miss Hammond's departure. Not for a long time, at least. Now Beatrix lived all alone on the third floor, although one of the underservants slept there too. Did her parents think she'd be afraid to stay alone at night? Beatrix wondered. Because that wasn't the kind of thing she feared at all.

During the day she managed to keep very busy. Frequently she walked over to the Kensington Museum, where her good friend, Miss Woodward, was always ready to help her. She continued to draw fungi. She filled notebook after notebook with her careful drawings, using Bertram's microscope to study the details of the little plants. After all, with thousands of species in the world, this could be a lifetime's work. She also made countless studies of rabbits and squirrels. There was her pet hedgehog Tiggy (whom she had brought back from Wray), that she drew in all different positions. The position she liked best was when he rolled himself into a tight spiney ball so that his enemies couldn't touch—let alone eat—him without being hurt themselves. Beatrix wished she could do the same. Not that she wanted to hurt anybody, but she did like being left alone.

Going to the Museum, continuing her studies of pressed leaves and flowers at home, taking care of Tiggy, her mice family, the pet rabbit she had brought back from the country, and the bats, drawing pictures, and reading any book she could borrow from the library was almost enough to fill out her days. But sometimes she still had time to think of people who weren't around her anymore, like Miss Hammond, and Mr. Cox, who had gone to live with his brother in America.

By now, Hunca Munca had had so many families of children that Beatrix had released many of them to run loose out-of-doors. In fact, she was never quite sure now which mice were parents, grandparents, or even great-grandparents. Anyway, a dear little pair was currently on the third floor. They might just possibly be the original Hunca and Appley.

The Nicest Boy

SO THE MONTHS WENT ON, each one as like the one before as beads on a string. There were some changes, of course. Beatrix was becoming a young lady, and she wore her hair up and her dresses long. She went down to the parlor for tea, and went visiting with her mother to various relatives. But she was so shy and quiet that no one noticed her very much.

One treat she enjoyed now was going to art exhibitions where she could study the work of famous painters. "I never thought there *could* be such pictures," she wrote in her journal. "It is almost too much to see them all at once—just fancy seeing five magnificent Van Dycks side by side, before *me* who never thought to see one."

Occasionally her father took her to art galleries, for Mr. Potter, as a photographer, was interested in art too. In fact, one of his good friends was the artist Millais, and Mr. Potter spent a good deal of time in Millais' studio, photographing his models. But Beatrix found him rather an uncomfortable companion sometimes. She once wrote in her journal:

I am sure he has not the least idea of the difficulty of painting a picture. He can draw well, but he has hardly attempted water color, and never oil. A person in this state, with a correct eye, and good taste, and great experience of different painters, sees all the failures and not the difficulties. Then, seeing Mr. Millais paint so often and so easily, would make a man hard on other painters. It prevents me showing much of my attempts to him, and I lose much by it.

Not for a minute did Beatrix think her life was odd or unhappy. She had never had companions of her own age, so did not miss them. What did suddenly become unbearable, though, was that she was made to go to dances given for some of her older cousins who came up to London from their country homes for a season of gay parties. Her parents insisted she go to these parties too. It was torture. Still, there was usually one chair that Beatrix could furtively push behind a large plant. There she would sit, reasonably safe from being discovered, until it was time to go home. Then, one evening, disaster! She had been quietly sitting behind a palm, as noiseless as Hunca Munca, when suddenly a voice startled her:

"Beatrix, *darling.* I've been looking all over for you! Come, dear, I want you to meet the nicest boy."

Wildly, Beatrix tried to find a way to escape. "I—I have to go home, Auntie D. At once."

"But the evening has hardly begun!"

"I—Our coachman is waiting. His—" with desperate inventiveness—"his wife is ill. I—I—"

But she was caught, and she knew it. And there was the "nicest boy," caught too. How terrible to have a girl dragged out from behind a potted palm to dance with him! Her dress wasn't the least bit like the other girls' dresses, either. Or her shoes.

But Beatrix knew she couldn't run away. That would look as though the boy had said something impolite to her and, stealing a glance at him, she could see he really was nice. Tall. Lean. Pink cheeks. Shining hair. After that first furtive peek, Beatrix didn't dare look again. Nothing for it but to let him put his long right arm around her waist and hold her right hand with his left.

He smiled down at her. Beatrix was a pretty girl, though small for her age. Her brown hair was soft and glossy. Her eyes were even bluer than Miss Ham-

mond's, and always very questioning.

"You shouldn't hide," the boy said. "Why did you do that?"

This was worse than trying to talk to her father. Beatrix wanted to say something nice to this boy, but what she blurted out was just awful.

"I have to."

"Have to hide? Why?"

"Because I'm frightened."

"Frightened of what?"

"People. Young ones especially. Thank you, though."

"For dancing with you?"

"Not so much that as for letting me go."

"Go? Are you ill?"

"No—but I must go. At once."

"Look. I—well, I understand girls. I have two sisters, Edith and Millie."

Later Beatrix was to think, if only she had had the courage to say to him, "I have a brother. His name is Bertram." Then maybe they could have talked about Bertram and the school he hated so much. Did all little boys hate boarding school, she could have asked the nicest boy. But what she actually said made Beatrix blush to the roots of her hair whenever she remembered it:

"This is dreadful. I must go. Good-bye."

On her way home that night, Beatrix threw up all over the inside of the beautifully upholstered carriage. The coachman reported this. Next morning Mrs. Potter sent for a doctor, but he could find nothing wrong with Beatrix. "Perhaps our friend should get out more in the sunshine," he said to Mrs. Potter, his glance traveling around the room. "She looks as though she were a bookworm. A pale little bookworm at that."

Mr. and Mrs. Potter never made their daughter go

to another dance. She was left to her quiet life in the third-floor schoolroom, drawing, visiting the Museum, working on her collections. As time passed, Beatrix began to wonder if her parents hadn't decided that it might be less trouble just to let her grow up in her own way. Apparently they had decided to ignore Benjamin Bunny, Tiggy, Hunca Munca, the bats, and Beatrix's other pets. At least, nothing was ever said about them.

Beatrix realized, and very much regretted, that she was becoming more and more shy and awkward with people. For instance, one afternoon a Mrs. Grant came for tea. She was the wife of a man who had taken Beatrix on some wonderful walks during their holidays in Scotland. Mrs. Potter sent Agnes, the parlormaid, to ask Beatrix to come downstairs.

"Well, now, not for anything in the world would I have missed seeing you, Beatrix. Goodness, if you haven't turned into a young lady!" said Mrs. Grant with an affectionate smile.

Beatrix knew that she should say something polite, and she wanted to, for she really liked Mrs. Grant. But she couldn't say a word. She swallowed hard several times in quick succession, and stood stiff and silent, allowing Mrs. Grant to take her hand as though it belonged to a limp rag doll. Beatrix hoped her mother didn't notice anything unusual—she so seldom noticed her daughter at all. But she couldn't be sure.

She might be deciding not to let anyone else see what a very queer daughter she had.

A few days later Beatrix overheard a conversation between her father and mother that gave her something else to think about. She was sitting quietly in the parlor, writing in her journal, when her mother and father came in without noticing her.

"My dear," her father was saying, "don't you think we should do something about having our daughter learn languages? German and French?"

Beatrix's mother agreed, adding, "She's never really had music lessons either, and we do have an excellent piano."

"I doubt if she has a talent for music," her father said thoughtfully. "It is drawing that seems to attract her. But French and German are acquirements every well-brought-up girl should have. And a governess could encourage her to be outdoors more, to take healthy walks. In spite of all those animals she thinks we do not know about, she is too solitary. We don't want her to get queer and stubborn—like those Cromptons my mother is always talking about."

"Goodness, no! But I don't think there's much danger of that when she's too shy even to say How-do-you-do to Mrs. Grant."

"Well," said Mr. Potter, "we can't be too careful."

Mademoiselle Meringue, the French governess who came soon afterwards, turned out to be a kind of Miss

Slaughter, only crosser and older, with a large hairy wart on her chin. There was one good thing about her, though; she was lazy. It was easy for Beatrix to persuade Mademoiselle Meringue to leave her at the Museum and call for her several hours later. Mademoiselle always had shopping to do, friends to visit, little restaurants where she enjoyed having coffee and hot milk instead of that awful British tea. But the day came when Beatrix's father, having asked his daughter a few simple questions, discovered that Beatrix hadn't learned any French beyond *"Comment ça va?"* *"Bon jour,"* *"J'aime ma mère,"* and *"J'aime beaucoup les animaux."*

In Mr. Potter's opinion, less than two dozen words of French were not enough for the amount he had already paid Mademoiselle Meringue for six weeks of teaching, so off she went and Beatrix heaved a vast sigh of relief, feeling it might be quite a while before her parents got around to hiring another governess. She was wrong. In less than two weeks Miss Annie Carter came.

Annie Carter
Takes Charge

MISS ANNIE CARTER was erect and thin and moved very quickly. She had long legs like a colt's. She often ran instead of walking, even if it was only to cross the room. Her hair was straight and brown, her eyes big and brown, too. Her hands were slim and graceful.

Just as Miss Hammond had before her, Miss Carter liked the sunny third floor rooms. She liked exercise, too. The very day she came, she wondered if they couldn't take *der Hase* (pronounced Haza) out for a stroll?

"*Haza?*" Beatrix repeated doubtfully.

"German for rabbit. *Er ist wunderbar.*"

Oh dear, thought Beatrix, nothing lazy about Miss Carter, she'd already begun speaking German. Beatrix didn't ask her what *er ist wunderbar* meant. But Miss Carter went right on.

"*Du liebst mich.* Let's try that before we start out for our walk."

Delighted that Benjamin Bunny was coming too, Beatrix tried hard.

"Surprisingly good except for the last word," said Miss Carter, tying a ribbon around Benjamin's neck. "That last word is pronounced *mich.* Not *mish.* Not *mick.* Not *mitch,* either. Say it exactly as I said it."

Very clearly Beatrix repeated: "*Du liebst mich.* What does it mean?"

"You love me," grinned Miss Annie Carter. "But I'm afraid your bunny doesn't love this leash of his." She held the squirming rabbit firmly with her strong hands. "All right, Benjamin, we'll try an outing another time. Anyway, we had better make a little jacket for you. It's cold outdoors these days." She untied the ribbon, put Benjamin on the floor, and told Beatrix not to be discouraged, he could be trained.

"And now shall we sing a song together? At least, let's start it, and then we can practice while we're walking. Ready?"

> "*Wir sind zwei kleine,*
> *Kleine, kleine biene:*
> *Ich bin der cousin,*
> *Du bist das cousinchen. . . ."*

"I like the tune," Beatrix said. "And I'll try to learn the words. But what do they mean?"

> "We are two lit-tle
> Tiny little bee-ees;
> I'm the big boy cousin,
> You're the darling she-ee. . . .

"A terrible translation," said Miss Annie Carter. "Never mind. Although I've never taught before, teaching is my job."

Beatrix said she had never felt that way about her cousins: that they were tiny bees. And she didn't think they ever thought about her at all.

"Oh, well, you may get around to liking one another. How old are you, Beatrix?"

"Sixteen—I'll be seventeen in July."

At Miss Annie Carter's look of amazement Beatrix said: "Don't you believe me?"

"Of course I believe you. But you do seem younger. I mean, I'm nineteen. But then I've been abroad. I studied in Germany. Have you been many places?"

"We used to go to Scotland for the summer holidays. Then we went to Wray Castle near Lake Windermere. This year we're going to Woodfield, near St. Albans. Can you come with us?"

"But summer won't be here for months, and by then . . ."

Miss Annie Carter paused. "Anyway, you must call me Annie, not Miss Carter, since I'm only three years older than you."

Beatrix wondered if she dared call a teacher, a governess, by her first name, but Annie Carter's brown eyes told her not to be afraid. Still, she needed time to get used to the idea.

To fill the silence Beatrix started with:

"Wir sind zwei kleine, kleine——"

She broke off, stuck for the words. "Oh, well, what we are is two little bees, buzz, buzz."
"Wunderbar."

As they walked up Queen's Gate, Beatrix told Annie Carter about the Kensington Museum of Natural History, and Annie Carter told Beatrix about another museum called the Victoria and Albert where, among other things, the most beautiful clothes were displayed as well as tapestries and embroideries. "You'll find the most marvelous flower and leaf designs there, and stitched portraits of all sorts of creatures, like Benjamin, *deine——?"*

"Hase, prounced Haza, German for rabbit," said Beatrix glibly, and smiled up at Annie's delight.

Annie was indeed pleased her pupil was proving to be bright. It might make that solemn pair, Mr. and Mrs. Potter, think she was a good teacher, and this was important because Annie needed to make money.

"Annie?" There, she'd said it! Beatrix thought proudly. Annie, my new friend, Annie.

"Yes, Beatrix?"

"You said—I remember exactly what you said— 'Summer won't be here for months, and then . . .' What did you mean? By then, you'll be doing what?'

"Going back home to Wandsworth," said Annie. "Please don't be upset, Beatrix. This governessing was only to last a few months, as I told your father when he engaged me. But I want us to go on being friends, and I hope you'll come to see me often. It's an easy drive over to Wandsworth, you know."

"My parents wouldn't let me," Beatrix said reluctantly.

"I think they will. You're just starting German, and we can keep up your lessons in my home. Besides, I gather from what I've heard that your father is worried about you."

"My father hardly ever sees me. If he is worried, he doesn't seem to do anything about it."

"I think he worries about your spending so much time alone."

"I don't mind being alone. Besides, I never really am."

"I know. You have your birds and your animals and your own self for company. And then of course you draw, you paint, you make collections. You learn a great deal by yourself."

"I like learning."

"But there's more to life than learning. Really there is, Beatrix."

"What?"

"Living," said Annie Carter. "You'll see."

With Annie's encouragement to prod her on, Beatrix did begin to go out more. She investigated the Victoria and Albert Museum, and was fascinated with the displays of beautiful tapestries and embroideries there. She went to art exhibits, and learned to look at paintings with a critical eye. But not even Annie could persuade her to go to dances or parties with her cousins. The memory of that last dance she had gone to still haunted her.

Annie planned to leave the Potters about the middle of June, and a few days before that date, she trapped Mr. Potter in his library, where he was lovingly turning the pages of his photograph album. Annie waited until he looked up before she spoke.

"Mr. Potter, I wanted to talk to you about Beatrix."

"About Beatrix?" Mr. Potter knit his heavy brows in displeasure.

"Yes. I am very fond of her, and I think she has an affection for me, too. Now, Mr. Potter, I would like to have her come to visit me when the summer holidays are over—as often as she likes. I am the only companion she has near her own age, and that is not natural, you know. At my home she could meet my brothers and sisters, and, perhaps, other young people. She may not mingle much, but at least she will have a look at life."

Mr. Potter continued to frown uneasily. "But will she want to go? You are aware as I am that Beatrix never sees anyone her own age, not even her cousins. She doesn't want to."

"But there may be harm in that," Annie pressed on, earnestly. "She may become so shy that you and Mrs. Potter could have a serious problem on your hands. She could become queer and eccentric. And what a pity, because Beatrix is a remarkably gifted girl, and a lovable one, too. But she needs to meet people. *And,*" Annie continued, with as much authority as she could bring to her voice, "I would also like to keep giving her German lessons. That would provide an excuse for her coming to see me. I won't be far away— just in Wandsworth."

"Too far to walk," said Mr. Potter, quickly.

"But not to drive."

"My dear Miss Carter, I assure you our coachman is an extremely busy man. He has no one to help him with keeping the horse groomed, the harness in good repair, the harness brass polished, the interior of the carriage fresh and clean—aside from all his driving duties."

"I was thinking of a pony," said Annie Carter.

Mr. Potter very evidently felt Miss Carter's wits had left her. Annie barely managed not to laugh out loud as she realized he thought she meant Beatrix should ride the pony. Quickly she explained there would also be a pony cart.

"But I've just told you . . ."

"I know. About the coachman's duties. But driving Beatrix need not be one of them. She can learn to drive herself. We've already talked about it. So may she come to visit me?"

Unwillingly, falteringly, Mr. Potter said yes. What was the world coming to, he wondered. Didn't he already have enough to worry about, with Bertram wanting to leave school and study painting?

After Annie had left, he got his hat and silver-topped cane. He badly needed the refuge of the Athenaeum Club. On his way out, he asked Agnes to inform Mrs. Potter he would not be home that evening.

The Years Go Marching On

SO ANNIE CARTER left in June, and in July the Potter family departed from London to spend the summer at Woodfield, where Beatrix thoroughly enjoyed herself watching and studying the farm animals. "There are two old cats and an amusing kitten," she wrote in her journal. "A cow, a heifer, and two calves, and two delightful pigs who lie on their backs, smiling sweetly to be scratched."

As soon as they returned to London, Beatrix went to call on Annie Carter in her pony cart. Mr. Potter, alarmed at Annie Carter's prophecy that his daughter might become "queer" and "eccentric" (like the Cromptons?) hadn't put up much of a battle over the pony, but both he and Mrs. Potter insisted that Beatrix should be accompanied by a maid wherever she went.

"What if I suggested that *he* drive me over in the pony cart?" Beatrix asked suddenly, as she and Annie were having tea in Annie's little parlor. Both girls doubled over with the giggles.

But Beatrix had more exciting news than the acquisition of the new pony.

"Just think, Annie, I'm to have lessons in oil painting—twelve of them—beginning tomorrow. Papa arranged it. I was so surprised when he told me! My teacher will be a Mrs. A—I forget the name—Ames, I think."

"Wonderful, my dear. But why just twelve?"

"Well, it seems Mrs. A's charges are quite high, and I suppose Papa thought that for a girl twelve lessons would be quite enough. It was Mr. Millais who gave him the idea, really. Papa and Mama took me to see him a few days ago. He was very kind about my drawing and suggested to Papa that I take some lessons with a Mrs. Ward. But Papa decided on Mrs. A. instead. I hope I'll like her."

"I hope so too. But haven't you had any lessons before?"

"Oh, yes. A Miss Cameron gave me drawing lessons off and on for several years. I have great reason to be grateful to her—she taught me freehand drawing, and perspective, and something about watercolor. Nothing in oils, though. But you know, Annie, painting is an awkward thing to teach. If a teacher and a pupil look at things in different ways—well, you are sure to have problems."

Annie laughed comfortably. "I know you will paint the way you like, my dear. Let's hope Mrs. A sees things your way."

But on Beatrix's next visit she seemed discouraged.

"I wouldn't say a word about it at home, of course," she confided, "but I don't much like Mrs. A. or her painting. She draws and paints pretty well, but it's all as smooth as a plate—no character, no life! Oh, dear, it is disappointing, when you do get some lessons, to be taught in a way you dislike and have to swallow your feelings!"

But the lessons came to an end and life went on much the same as always at Number Two Bolton Gardens. Bertram was away at school, and so Beatrix was alone on the third floor, except for her pets, of course. On December 8 she wrote about her family of snails:

An awful tragedy discovered. The whole Bill family—old Bill and Mrs. Little Bill, and ditto Grimes and Sextus Grimes his wife, Lord and Lady Salisbury, Mr. and Mrs. Campfield, Mars

*and Venus, and three or four others were every
one dead and dried up. We have had old Bill
more than a year. I am very much put out about
the poor things, they have such a surprising dif-
ference of character, and besides it was partly our
fault, but they were all asleep in bed and it
seemed cruel to water them.*

The next summer, before they left for their summer
vacation, Mr. and Mrs. Potter and Beatrix went to
visit Grandmother Potter, who was now an old lady
of eighty-four. Beatrix wrote of her affectionately:

*How pretty she does look with her grey curls,
under her muslin cap, trimmed with black lace.
Her plain crepe dress with broad grey linen collar
and cuffs turned over. So erect and always on the
move, with her gentle face and waken twinkling
eyes. There is no one like Grandmamma. She always seems to me as near perfect as is possible
here.*

Beatrix remembered now something her grandmother had said about change: that nothing remained
the same. Every single day a person lived, he or she
grew older. That, in itself, was change.

They returned to London in October, as usual, and

Beatrix waited hopefully to see if anything would be said about her painting, but the subject was not mentioned.

There's not a word about my painting just now (she wrote), and I don't want any except for more time. I don't want lessons, I want practice. I hope it is not pride that makes me so stiff against teaching, but a bad or indifferent teacher is worse than none.

Now Beatrix was edging toward being nineteen. On July 9 of that year she wrote: "My education is finished. Whatever moral good and general knowledge I may have got from it, I have retained no literal rules. I don't believe I can repeat a single line of any language. . . . I regret French very much, history I can read alone, German is still going on, the rules of geography and grammar are tiresome, there is no general word to express the feelings I have always entertained towards arithmetic!"

The next four or five years passed with little to mark them, except that Annie Carter married a Mr. William Moore, and a year later produced an eight-pound son. He was named Noel.

During these years, too, Beatrix was quite ill for a time, possibly with rheumatic fever, and could not paint or write in her journal for many weeks. Slowly she struggled back to health again, and life went on at Number Two much as usual.

Just before she was twenty-four, Bertram, in spite of all his rebelling, actually finished his last year at school. He was still determined to be a painter, but instead of going to art school, which would have horrified his parents—live lady models and possibly even a wicked studio in Paris!—he continued to live at home, as self-taught as his sister. But how different his painting was from hers! Beatrix loved the tiny, precise details of flowers or mushrooms or small animals, and Bertram liked to cover his canvasses with huge landscapes. Soon, using his frugally saved allowance, Bertram was spending considerable time in Scotland, painting jagged mountains, roaring rivers, tall, crooked trees.

During this year though, Beatrix and Bertram put their heads together and, greatly daring, decided to send some Christmas card designs to a publisher. Beatrix made up six designs, using her pet rabbit, Benjamin Bouncer, as a model, and they got the addresses of six publishers to send them to. The first publisher sent them back immediately, but the second actually wrote and asked to see some more sketches! Trembling with shyness and excitement, Beatrix went to see him, accompanied by her uncle, and taking some additional sketches. But the visit was a disappointment, for the publisher wanted her to do drawings to order and in his style, which she did not feel she could do. "He did not strike me as being a person of much taste," she wrote in her journal. "In fact, he rather gave me to understand, when I objected to drawing such and such an animal, that it was the humor that signified, not the likeness."

Beatrix missed Bertram during his frequent trips to Scotland, but the Moore family proved a wonderful compensation. Annie Moore's babies came quite regularly. With so many mouths to feed, Annie was pleased to continue earning some money by teaching Beatrix. The German lessons went on indefinitely.

Each of Annie's babies was as rosy and cheerful as the last. They all loved Beatrix.

These days when Beatrix went away with her parents for the summer holidays, she boldly took her animals along. This her parents ignored. With time, her pets had changed in species and appearance, although Beatrix had not. She still wore the same long serge skirts she had worn at fifteen, though now, on Sundays, she might wear a dress with a bustle. When traveling, she always carried an umbrella, a rabbit hutch, and a great array of boxes and baskets. There was a special box for Hunca and a basket for the hedgehog, Tiggy. She wrote in her journal about Tiggy: "My hedgehog enjoys the train. She is always very hungry when she's on a journey." And about her rabbit: "Benjamin Bunny traveled in a covered basket in the wash-place; took him out of the basket near Dunbar, but he proved scared and bit the family."

When Bertram went back and forth to Scotland, he traveled with pets too, even odder ones than his sis-

ter's. A Barbary falcon, for instance, who used to sit on Bertram's head and lean over to peck food off his plate. Naturally, this only happened when Bertram and Beatrix were having a private meal together, which was seldom.

There came a surprising time when Beatrix was actually happy about a departing pet of Bertram's: an owl. Bertram took him to Scotland and never brought him back. At Number Two this owl had hooted all night. And when, on occasion, he had caught a mouse, he would devour it whole, except for its tail, which dangled gruesomely out of his mouth. Bertram, in fact, seemed to have a liking for troublesome pets. At another time Beatrix wrote: "Bertram went away to Oxford on the morning with the Jay crammed into a little wooden box, kicking and swearing. Mamma expressed her uncharitable hope that we might have seen the last of it. It is an entertaining, handsome bird, but unsuitable for the house."

The Potters continued to spend their summers in various parts of the country, usually in the Lake District. Whenever Beatrix and Canon Rawnsley happened to meet during the summers, they had a delightful time together.

"How wonderful to see you again, my dear Miss Mycologist," the Canon would say, shaking hands.

"Now please don't ask me about that mushroom book! I'm afraid it could only be a very slim one.

"So kindly tell me why you can't make it longer?"

"Because I only like a few of the drawings I've made. Oh, I've done dozens—hundreds! But only a few seem good enough for a book. And then I keep getting interested in so many other things. I've done our bats. And of course cats and mice and squirrels and sheep and cows and rabbits and frogs and lots of flower and vegetable gardens and the insides of kitchens and bedrooms—and can you guess what else?"

The Canon couldn't.

"I've begun drawing clothes on my animals! Clothes that seem right for each particular animal. For instance, mice have always seemed such housekeeping little creatures to me. So sometimes a lady mouse needs an apron, and I'm sure she likes to rock her nightgowned babies in a cradle. And sometimes it really has been necessary for me to put a jacket on a rabbit. . . . I hope you don't think this sounds silly."

"I think it sounds delightful. Have you any of these pictures with you?"

"Yes, a few. However, I will keep on with my mushrooms. I promise. Perhaps they can be used to illustrate a book about mushrooms, someday. I must tell you, though, that a botany man at the Museum said my mushroom pictures didn't have enough precise scientific detail."

"But the detail you could learn by studying and, in my opinion, you have something more important: a feeling of the earthiness of mushrooms. The moss and grass and fallen leaves around them. Remember that fairy ring you did?"

"When Miss Hammond was with me? The *Clitocyle cerusa*? They grow in coniferous woods and deciduous parks. And speaking of woods, can you imagine what Bertram is trying to do in Scotland now? He wrote me he was trying to paint the smell of heather."

"Is that where Bertram is now? Scotland?"

"Yes. He wants to buy a farm and live there."

"Won't that be lonesome for him?"

"No, I think not. He likes farm life."

"For you, then?"

"Well, my parents are going to let me visit him if he does buy a farm. And as you know, I see the Moore family all the time. Five children now. But Canon Rawnsley, what have *you* been doing?"

The Canon chuckled. "Not letting people build horrid bungalows in this beautiful countryside. Nor permitting railroads anywhere near here. Nor letting them tear down our picturesque old bridges and build cheap new ones. Not allowing objectionable postcards to be printed. Oh, I'm a terror. City councils and committees tremble at the sight of my old gray beard."

Beatrix laughed. "I can well believe it! How many bonfires was it you lit when Queen Victoria had her jubilee?"

"One hundred and forty-eight. I was hoping for one hundred and fifty."

In her stout boots, Beatrix stood on tiptoe and kissed the Canon on his cheek. "They must have been beautiful," she said. "I wish I'd seen them."

Later Beatrix showed the Canon her drawings of animals in clothes. He studied them carefully. "To tell the truth," he said, "I wasn't sure I'd like them. But I do. I like them very much. Why don't you fit them into a book?"

"Instead of the mushrooms?"

"No. But maybe before the mushrooms. That is, if you have a feeling for doing them. How old are you, Beatrix?"

"Twenty-six my next birthday."

"Old enough to build yourself a raft. You have everything you need: imagination, determination, talent. Build a raft and paddle away. Bertram has done it, and he's younger."

"But he's a boy."

"Bosh! Girls are just as good as boys."

Beatrix hesitated shyly. "Well, do you know, I *have* sold one drawing—a drawing of a jackdaw."

"There, you see!" the Canon beamed. "You've made the first step out of the nest. Who knows what may be next? A whole book of drawings, perhaps!"

"Papa and Mama wouldn't like it, I'm afraid."

"We'll see about that!" said the Canon, robustly.

Nothing more was said, but a few months later Beatrix was invited to illustrate a tiny booklet of verses by Frederic E. Wetherby, a friend of the Canon's and slightly known to Mr. Potter, too. *The Happy Pair*, it was called. Beatrix felt quite at home with it, for the pictures were all of rabbits. One of them especially made her chuckle as she drew the rabbit on a railway platform, surrounded with boxes, carpetbag, and umbrella—so like herself when traveling:

> My name's Mr. Benjamin Bunny
> And I travel about without money.
> There are lots I could name
> Do precisely the same,
> It's convenient, but certainly funny.

A Letter To Noel

ON THE MORNING OF A BRIGHT hot day in September in the year when Beatrix Potter became twenty-seven, she received a letter from her friend Annie Moore saying that her oldest child, Noel, (whose birthday was the same as Beatrix's), had come down with rheumatic fever and would have to be kept quiet for many months.

Can you imagine a five-year-old being tied down to his bed? He's been good about it so far. His father is wonderful at thinking up games for him to play, but I know we can't continue this pace of keeping him occupied. Besides killing us, it might turn Noel into a spoiled and demanding

*little boy. He'll have to learn to entertain himself.
Although tempted to, I haven't given him your
birthday present yet. I try to spread out his treats.*

Beatrix went straight to her room and began a
letter:

My dear Noel——

*I don't know what to write you, so I shall tell
you a story about four little rabbits whose names
were Flopsy, Mopsy, Cottontail, and Peter. They
lived with their mother in a sandbank under the
roots of a big tree . . . "Now, my dears," said
old Mrs. Bunny, "you may go into the field or
down the lane, but don't go into Mr. McGregor's
garden . . ."*

The illustration on the first page of Beatrix Potter's
letter was of the four little rabbits. Three of them—
Flopsy, Mopsy, and Peter—had pricked-up ears, but
Cottontail had folded her ears back. She looked comfortable and sleepy that way. Peter's ears were the
most alert and listening. Old Mrs. Bunny looked like
a worried mother who hoped her children would be-
have but was not at all certain they would.

On the second page of the letter each small rabbit
was wearing a jacket. Old Mrs. Bunny, with an apron

tied around her waist, was handing her children a basket in which to put the wild blackberries she had asked them to pick for supper.

Off they went.

Flopsy, Mopsy, and Cottontail were good, obedient little rabbits and began picking blackberries, but Peter got into serious trouble immediately. He bounded into Mr. McGregor's garden where he ate lettuce, beans, and radishes. For fear of getting caught by Mr. Mc-Gregor, he ate too much and too quickly. That gave him a terrible stomachache which sent him hunting for parsley. His mother insisted parsley was the best cure for indigestion. But, just as he was coming around the corner of a cucumber frame, what awful sight did he see? Mr. McGregor, chasing him with a rake!

Peter ran as fast as he could, and as he ran, he lost both shoes. But that wasn't the worst. One of the large brass buttons on his jacket got caught in a net draped around a gooseberry bush to protect it from greedy birds. Peter's jacket was blue and quite new. But in order to escape from Mr. McGregor, he had to wriggle out of it and leave it on the bush. When he arrived home without his shoes and his coat, his mother punished him by putting him to bed. She made him drink camomile tea, but Flopsy, Mopsy, and Cottontail had bread and milk and blackberries for their supper.

Beatrix finished off her letter by saying she was coming back to London on Thursday. "So I shall soon be seeing you and the new baby. I remain, yours affectionately, Beatrix Potter."

This letter to Noel was the first of many little stories Beatrix wrote to the Moore children, illustrated with pen-and-ink sketches. The following summer, when Eric Moore was having mumps in London, she wrote him about a frog named Jeremy Fisher "who lived in a little house on the bank of a river," and who "liked getting his feet wet, nobody ever scolded him, and he never caught cold." She wrote Norah Moore about a mischievous little squirrel called Squirrel Nutkin, and how he lost his tail. She wrote about a cat named Tabitha Twitchet, "who was an anxious parent," always losing her kittens. On a visit to her cousin Caroline Hutton in Gloucester, she heard a story about a tailor who had left a coat cut out one night and found it mysteriously finished in the morning, and this so fascinated her that she wove a story about the tailor which she sent to little Freda Moore with a letter:

My dear Freda:

Because you are fond of fairy tales, and have been ill, I have made you a story all for yourself— a new one that nobody had heard before.

Needless to say, the children were delighted.

Seven more years went by. Beatrix continued working in the two museums. She went to art exhibitions. She collected and painted mushrooms. She collected fossils, too, during summer holidays, and took up her father's hobby of photography. But where he usually photographed his friends and well-to-do acquaintances, she liked to take pictures of animals and country scenes

and farm cottages. Twice she visited her brother in
Scotland, where Bertram still caught terrible colds
but didn't mind because he loved the Scottish country so much. He had two good servants who took care
of him. He farmed. He painted. Beatrix envied him
his independence.

All these activities kept her very busy. At the end of
one summer's holiday she wrote:

> *I am very sorry indeed to come away, but I have
> done a good summer's work. . . . My photography
> was not satisfactory, but I made about forty care-
> ful drawings of funguses and collected some in-
> teresting fossils. . . . For the rest, I read sundry
> old novels, some of which I had read before. I
> also learned four acts of* Henry VIII *and meant
> to have learned all, but I can say this for my
> diligence, that every line was learnt in bed. . . . I
> know* Richard III *right through,* Henry VI, *four-
> fifths;* Richard II *except three pages;* King John
> *four acts, a good half of the* Midsummer Night's
> Dream *and* The Tempest, *and half way through
> the* Merchant of Venice. *I learnt six more or less
> in a year. Never felt the least strained or should
> not have done it.*

Canon Rawnsley, when he saw her, still called her
Miss Mycologist, but he had given up begging her to

do the mushroom book. They both realized this would take more scientific training than she had. She did send a paper on the "Germination of the Spores of Agaricineae" to the Linnaean Society when she was thirty-one years old, but she did not read it herself.

But now Canon Rawnsley was asking her why she didn't do what he had suggested a long time ago: make a book of her dressed-up animal characters?

Beatrix became interested. She remembered how the Moore children had loved the animal pictures she had sent them in letters. Perhaps it was natural for children to like pictures of little animals.

"Do stories go with the pictures?" the Canon asked her.

"Mostly."

"Which pictures and story do you like the best?"

"Well, perhaps the one about Peter Rabbit that I wrote for little Noel Moore."

"Then put the story and pictures into shape and I'll give you the name of a publisher."

"A *publisher*! Goodness! But, oh dear."

"Oh dear what?"

"I just don't think it's likely Noel would have kept that story about Peter Rabbit. After all, I wrote him that letter—let's see now—about eight years ago."

"Find out," said the Canon.

Beatrix wrote to Noel immediately and he wrote

back. Of course he had kept the letter about Peter. He had kept all her letters.

A month later, Beatrix sent *The Tale of Peter Rabbit* to seven publishers, one after another. All seven turned it down. However, one publisher, Frederick Warne & Company, wrote a polite and even slightly encouraging letter with their refusal.

Still, a refusal it was.

So Beatrix decided to be her own publisher. Encouraged by Canon Rawnsley, she drew what seemed like a very large sum out of her Post Office savings account, and got in touch with a printer whose name was given to her by Miss Woodward. The book should be small, Beatrix decided, with only one or two sentences on each page and a picture every time a page was turned over.

Except for being somewhat longer, the book turned out to be almost exactly like her letter to Noel. There was one picture washed with color: this was old Mrs. Bunny administering camomile tea to her disobedient son. The other pictures were all black and white.

A Bell: Ding Dong

PEOPLE ACTUALLY BOUGHT Beatrix's book. After clearing expenses, she made fourteen pounds selling *Peter Rabbit* to her aunts and other relations at one shilling twopence a copy. The aunts showed *Peter* to friends and children of friends, and they bought books. Beatrix sent a copy to Miss Hammond, and Miss Hammond's friends bought *Peter*. A bookshop in Kensington wanted to put copies of *Peter Rabbit* in their store window, but Beatrix felt shy about this. The first edition of two hundred and fifty copies melted away. Beatrix began to think of getting out another edition; but before she had talked to her printer about this, a letter came from the publishers Frederick Warne & Company offering to publish *Peter Rabbit* if she

would do the illustrations in color. This letter was
signed by Norman Warne, one of the three brothers
who made up the firm.

Beatrix's elation was quickly dampened by her
father. Mr. Potter distrusted publishers. After all, publishers were in trade, in business! Businessmen were
distasteful to Mr. Potter. They were too sharp, too
shrewd. This Frederick Warne & Company, what
were they planning to get out of *his* daughter?

"But Papa, it was Canon Rawnsley who suggested
Warne's in the first place!" Beatrix protested.

This silenced Mr. Potter. Temporarily. Still, the
first letter Beatrix wrote to Mr. Norman Warne was
an uncertain one. She would be willing to re-draw the
whole book, if desired. She had not drawn the pictures in color originally, except the one of old Mrs.
Bunny, for two reasons: "The expense of good color
and also the rather uninteresting color of a good many
of my subjects, which are mostly rabbit brown or the
green of garden vegetables."

Beatrix went on to say that threepence apiece seemed
a generous royalty, but then, to whom would the
copyright belong? . . . "I am sure that such a small
book, even if successful, can't last long, but I should
like to know to what I am agreeing." And then, in a
most uncharacteristic outburst: "Sirs, it would be well
to explain the Agreement clearly because my father is
a little formal, having been trained as a barrister."

Norman Warne answered her letter, asking her to call so they could discuss the details. Beatrix replied: "Dear Sir, I am very sorry that I cannot call as I am going to Scotland tomorrow morning; my brother has made his arrangements, and I don't want to miss traveling with him. . . . I think I could very likely do them [the drawings] better there, as there is a garden. Would you be so kind as to post me the two that are the worst?"

Being with Bertram on his farm, away from her suspicious father, proved wonderful. Every detail of Bertram's garden, flowers, fences, and fields, seemed washed over with magic. Beatrix couldn't get them down on paper quickly enough. She became happier with her colors. One beautiful day followed another, fresh and blue. No rain! Such mists as dimmed the early mornings were soon sent scudding by the sun. Even the tops of the hills were emerald green.

Bertram, amused by his sister and proud of her, nevertheless teased her about Mr. McGregor. Animals were easy for her, humans were not. From Bertram's farm, Beatrix wrote to Norman Warne: "My brother is sarcastic about Mr. McGregor. What you and he take for one of Mr. McGregor's ears was intended to be his nose."

Beatrix added that her brother had offered to take photographs of his own farmer chasing Peter, rake in hand, so she could copy the photographs.

For many weeks there was a criss-crossing of letters: anxious ones from Beatrix, reassuring ones from Norman Warne. When Beatrix finally returned to London, she made a momentous decision—she would go to see her publisher, even though she knew her parents disapproved. She would show something of the Crompton spirit her grandmother had talked about.

In the office of Frederick Warne & Company she met Harold Warne, Fruing Warne, and Norman Warne. Although Beatrix was painfully shy, the three men helped her to feel at ease and there followed talk about the Agreement. Beatrix warned them her father might insist on coming to see the Agreement himself, and if he did, would they please not mind very much if he was fidgety. "In fact," she said, "I think it better to mention beforehand, he is difficult. I can, of course, do what I like about the book, being of age." Silently she added to herself, "And a Crompton!"

Soon after this business conference, she had a note from Norman Warne asking her to come for tea to his mother's house in Bedford Square. Without saying anything to her mother, she accepted. She drove to Bedford Square in the pony cart, without a maid. She was amazed and terrified by her own courage, but as soon as she found herself in that sunny big old house, so full of comfort and happiness, she felt as she did at the Moores': at home.

At home, but still timid.

Besides Mrs. Warne, the only other Warnes who lived at home were Norman and Millie, but that afternoon, another married sister called. This was Edith, trailed by two of her children. The children, a girl of seven and a boy of eight, began talking to Beatrix. They chattered on about their pets, and so Beatrix told them about Hunca Munca, Tiggy, Peter—even the minnows she had kept alive on train journeys by squirting air into their bottle. The three of them were gossiping away like old friends when suddenly a bell began ringing in Beatrix's memory. It seemed impossible at first that such an amazing coincidence should be, but as Beatrix focussed her mind on that memory, the Warne family seemed to disappear, their voices faded away. . . . She was back in the past, at a dancing party. Once again she heard her aunt saying:

"Beatrix, darling, I've been looking all over for you. I want you to meet the nicest boy."

"I have to go home, Auntie D."

"But the evening has hardly begun."

"I—our coachman is waiting. . . ."

Then the nicest boy was dutifully putting his arm about her waist, the nicest boy was saying, she shouldn't have hidden, why had she hid behind a potted plant?

Remembering her reply, Beatrix turned crimson, and stole a quick look at the tall, lean man beside her. Did Norman Warne suspect this extraordinary thing

she was now suspecting? She knew she hadn't changed very much in appearance since those school-girl days. Her hair was fixed the same old way; her face was much the same. Now, quite clearly above the cheerful conversation in the Bedford House parlor, she seemed to hear a young voice saying:

"Look, I—well, I understand girls. I have two sisters, Edith and Millie."

However wild this surmise might be, still here was a man about the right age, about the right height, with the look of gentleness Beatrix remembered. His cheeks weren't boyishly pink now, nor was his hair shining. Instead, it was thinning. Still, right in the room were two sisters named Edith and Millie. Well, thought Beatrix, this is something I haven't the courage to uncover; it would be like tearing the bandage off a wound.

When Edith left with her children, Beatrix rose to go, too. Gratefully she said good-bye to Mrs. Warne. As she shook hands with Millie, instinct told Beatrix that Millie was as bashful as she: a strange thing—trying to put someone *else* at ease. The two women shook hands warmly, gazing straight into each other's eyes.

Norman Warne accompanied Beatrix to her pony cart. Clover was tied to the hitching post directly in front of the house. Norman unhitched him, patted him on the nose, handed Beatrix the reins, removed Clover's blanket, folded it neatly, placed it across from Beatrix on the cart's long seat and thanked Beatrix for coming.

Beatrix blushed. "I enjoyed myself. I love your home. I hope . . ." she faltered, "to see your family again."

"Good. In fact, excellent. It's lovely to know you've come out from behind that potted plant."

No Santa Claus
That Year

NOW, IN TWO HOMES, Beatrix felt as though she were swimming in friendly waters.

Annie Moore had her sixth baby. Beatrix rejoiced with her.

Beatrix met all Mrs. Warne's grandchildren and learned how affectionately they felt toward their Uncle Norman. It was he who was always the bearded, red-robed, generously-stomached Santa Claus on Christmas Day. The older children guarded this secret conscientiously, but there was always someone just old enough to have been a believer the year before. "Why, it's Uncle Norman!" he or she would cry with out-stretched arms.

The year *Peter Rabbit* came out in color it was an

121

immediate success. Uncle Norman undertook to be Peter at the family Easter party, blue jacket, brass buttons, and all. He reported to Beatrix how professionally he'd twitched his pink-lined ears.

Beatrix, of course, was never around for these family occasions, but bit by bit, encouraged by success, she was beginning to assert herself in small ways.

The nursery bars at her bedroom windows were removed. She began to have friends for tea on the third floor. At first Mr. and Mrs. Potter assented only to adults, but gradually children started whispering and giggling their way up the back stairs. Beatrix wished Mr. Cox could hear these sounds. She had sent him a copy of *Peter Rabbit*, and he had written a most astonishing letter, first thanking her for the little book, saying it certainly should be published in America, and ending up with the news that he was married. "I have a little boy," he wrote. "When we have a little girl, her name will be Beatrix."

In the meantime Freda Moore and the other young Moores were begging for new stories. And as a matter of fact, Beatrix was feeling unhappy without something before her to work on. Once more she thought of the picture letters she had written the Moores. There was the Squirrel Nutkin story, which the children had liked so much, but especially there was the story of the Tailor of Gloucester and the mice who had finished the Lord Mayor's coat for him. Years be-

fore, while visiting her cousin, Caroline Hutton, in
Gloucester, Beatrix had actually seen just the right
tailor working in his cluttered little shop, and had
made a number of sketches of him.

The more she thought about the story, the more it
grew in her mind, but she was shy about sending it
to the Warnes. They might just think it silly, she
thought, or they might want to change it. So she
printed it privately herself, and then, just before
Christmas, sent a copy to Norman Warne. In an
accompanying letter she said she had undertaken the
book with courage, but now that it was done, was not
sure that it was satisfactory. A few days later she
wrote again:

> Thank you for your prompt letter about the
> mouse book. I think your criticisms are fair and
> after all you did pay me the compliment of tak-
> ing the plot seriously. . . . I was quite sure in
> advance that you would cut out the tailor and all
> my favorite rhymes! Alas, as things stand right
> now, my Tailor is mostly popular with very old
> ladies.

Shortly after that, on one of her visits to Bedford
House—Clover knew the way now, almost without
any guiding—she confided to Norman Warne that it
might improve the book if she cut the tailor out of

the illustrations. His wonderful shop, with the mice working on the embroidered coat and waistcoat, might be all she needed for the story. She could get the details for the embroidery at the Victoria and Albert Museum.

And so the matter rested for the moment. But churning around in Beatrix's mind there was a frog called Jeremy Fisher, a duck called Jemima Puddle-duck, Mrs. Tiggy-Winkle, the hedgehog, Benjamin Bunny (a cousin of Peter Rabbit), Squirrel Nutkin. These creatures wouldn't let her alone. They were with her wherever she went. In this somewhat frantic state of mind she started *The Tale of Squirrel Nutkin*.

Halfway through she tried it out on the Moores and a number of Mrs. Warne's grandchildren. They loved the pictures of the squirrels sailing across the lake to Old Mr. Brown's island on little rafts, using their tails for sails. One very small child was alarmed by Old Mr. Brown, the owl who sternly ruled the squirrels on his island, and who snipped off Nutkin's tail for teasing him. So Beatrix made the owl less ferocious.

Actually, Old Mr. Brown was Bertram's horrid owl who used to sit with a devoured mouse's tail dangling out of his mouth.

In time Warne's published *The Tale of Squirrel*

Nutkin, and also a revised and improved edition of *The Tailor of Gloucester. The Tale of Benjamin Bunny,* a sequel to *Peter Rabbit,* soon followed.

Some time later, Beatrix wrote Norman Warne she wished another book could be planned before summer. "I do so hate finishing books, I feel so lost when the work is closed," she wrote him.

Honest with herself, Beatrix knew she would also hate not corresponding with Norman; even more, not seeing him. His understanding, his kindness when he felt he must criticize, his good sense in business matters, gave her strength. Together they worked out the story for *The Tale of Two Bad Mice,* which was based partly on the mischievous activities of two of Beatrix's pet mice—Hunca Munca and Tom Thumb. To make her drawings for this book, Beatrix needed a house with a glass front, so she could watch the mice inside it. It was Norman who provided the mouse house, and also the doll-size furnishings—even a doll's-size ham for the kitchen that those two bad mice would raid.

The house was a delight to Beatrix as well as to her two mice, who loved scurrying up and down the ladder to their nest at the top. Unfortunately, the house was also, some time later, the setting for a sad event. Beatrix had trained her most recent Hunca to climb by easy stages up various pieces of furniture to the chandelier in Beatrix's bedroom, and then to jump, landing on a sofa. One day, instead of jumping, Hunca fell backwards. Beatrix wrote to Norman Warne:

I cannot forgive myself for letting her tumble. I do miss her so. Desperately in need of her nest, she managed to stagger up the staircase in your little house, but she died in my hands about ten minutes later. I think if I had broken my own neck it would have saved a great deal of trouble.

Norman comforted her as best he could, and the friendship between them became even stronger. *The Tale of Two Bad Mice* was followed a year later by *The Tale of Mrs. Tiggy-Winkle,* and Beatrix found the illustrations for this book turning out to be "very comical." Since her own pet hedgehog was too fat and sleepy to make a good model, she used a dressed-up dummy—"such a little figure of fun," she wrote, "it terrified my rabbit."

But while these cheerful projects jogged along, Mr. and Mrs. Potter were beginning to feel they had allowed their daughter too much freedom. All those visits to Bedford Street! All those letters from Norman Warne! Besides, she was straining her eyes over her drawings. But their real fear was that she was getting much too independent. Could it be she was earning too much money? Had they, her parents, not been sufficiently strict?

Both, they decided. A stop must be put to these activities. They could not very well nail back the nursery bars, but they could certainly forbid her to call at her publishers' office and at Mr. Warne's house. They could insist on her coming with them as usual for the summer holidays.

A subdued Beatrix wrote to the Warnes: "I cannot call at the office before leaving town. I have had painful unpleasantness at home. Please say no more about the new book."

But Norman Warne, by nature a slow and patient man, became impatient. After all, he and Beatrix had been seeing one another steadily for nearly four years. They were certainly old enough to know their own minds. He wrote a long letter to Beatrix, expressing his feelings for her and his wish to make her his wife.

Beatrix read the letter with both joy and dismay, torn between her feeling of duty towards her parents and an even stronger emotion. She realized that she had fallen in love.

During the summer she discussed her dilemma with Canon Rawnsley. In July, she became engaged to marry Norman. She wore his ring. When confronted with her decision, her parents, as she feared, exploded with indignation. Though they had half expected, and feared, such a development, they acted as though she was confronting them with a cruel shock. Become at-

tached to a man in *trade?* Go against her parents'
wishes? How could she!

But Beatrix was quietly obstinate.

"I'm sorry, Mama. I'm very sorry, Papa."

"You can't mean you are going ahead with this,
that you are planning to——"

"Marry Norman. Yes, I am."

"This is disgraceful."

"I'm sorry you think so."

"After all we've done for you!" said Mr. Potter.

Beatrix's temper suddenly blazed with something
of her grandmother's spirit.

"Keeping me in prison? Not ever being interested
in my work? Stunting me in every way you could?

Why I, why I——"

Beatrix didn't know what wild thing she might have said next. But as she groped for words to hurt her selfish, unimaginative parents, she suddenly saw something else about them too: they were old and frightened. Frightened perhaps of being left alone, now that Bertram had escaped to Scotland.

Beatrix had another startling idea: Might it be possible that her success had somehow made them feel uncertain of themselves? That they were behaving in this dreadful way to bolster up their own feelings of importance?

She tried to think how Norman Warne would act in such a situation.

"Please don't feel this way," she said gently to her parents. "It isn't as though I were never going to see you again. Why, Norman and I will be here often."

Norman and I will be here often. These words were the last straw for the Potters. They stalked from the room.

The words also turned out to be not true. Never a very strong man, Norman fell ill. He refused to talk about his illness, refused to consult a doctor. When he finally did, it was too late. He died on August 25.

There was no Santa Claus at Bedford House that year.

A New Beginning

BEATRIX WAS NEVER TO KNOW how her parents felt about Norman's death. The matter was never discussed between them. Perhaps they considered it a fortunate solution of the problem. At least, they acted as though nothing had happened; that everything was just the same as before.

As Beatrix struggled alone with her grief through the following weeks and months, she sometimes wondered how it had been when *they* were engaged. Had they ever felt any tenderness toward each other? Had they ever shared jokes? Had they missed each other when they were apart?

At last Beatrix gave up such odd speculations.

Days at Number Two ticked away in their usual

orderly fashion: In the mornings the Athenaeum Club for Mr. Potter; planning meals and writing letters for Mrs. Potter. After lunch, a drive together, unless Mr. Potter became involved in a game of cribbage or back-gammon at his club. Occasionally, a few errands. Every once in a while Mrs. Potter would ask Beatrix if she would like to join her in making calls, but Beatrix replied politely, Thank you, she thought not.

Beatrix still had tea in the nursery, but she now ate dinner with her parents. These days Mr. Muggins waited on table, a sad substitute for Mr. Cox. As he passed roast beef on a silver platter, or potatoes in a silver dish, Beatrix tried to imagine Mr. Muggins taking care of Hunca Munca's "traces," or helping her and Bertram organize a "Museum."

She knew she was fortunate to have another book to work on, to occupy her mind. It was *The Tale of Jeremy Fisher*, another one of the picture letters she had written to the Moore children years before, and had discussed with Norman. As she wrote and revised the story, drew and improved her drawings, Beatrix was beginning, not to recover exactly, but to feel calmer and more at peace. She wrote to Millie Warne: "He did not live long, but he fulfilled a useful and happy life. I must try to make a fresh beginning. He would want me to."

While Beatrix pondered this fresh beginning she did, of course, often drive over to see the Moores. The latest baby was the prettiest of all, a little girl with bright red hair.

"*Wunderbar*," Beatrix would murmur, nuzzling the tiny thing.

"*Ausgezeichnet?*"

"*Ja wohl!*"

This silly bit of dialog accompanied by gestures went on between Beatrix and Annie Moore for weeks. The baby seemed to enjoy it.

Although the Warnes often urged her to visit them, Beatrix, to her embarrassment and shame, could not bring herself to go. So far she had kept her feelings under strict control, but might not too many memories overwhelm her at Bedford House?

At last she got up her courage and went. As she drove, she really had to laugh at Clover; he seemed glad to be on that route again.

And she herself was glad she went. A smiling Mrs. Warne, wearing her white cap with lavender ribbons, Fruing and his wife Edith, the Harold Warnes, and of course Millie, along with a scattering of children, were all in the living room to greet Beatrix when she arrived. The afternoon was normal and easy. It seemed to Beatrix the whole family assumed Norman was still around and always would be. No need to fear she might have broken down. This was a supporting family. She could talk to them freely, knowing they would understand.

The same summer she had become engaged to Norman, Beatrix, with no one's support or advice, had made another bold decision. During the annual vacation in the Lake Country, she had heard of a farm for sale in the nearby village of Sawrey. Beatrix had always liked Sawrey. Years before she had written in her journal:

> It is as nearly perfect a little place as I ever lived in, and such nice old-fashioned people in the village. . . . I think one of my pleasantest memories is sitting on Oatmeal Crag on a Sunday afternoon, where there is a sort of table of rock with a cup, with the lane and fields and oak copse like in a trough below my feet, and all the tiny fungus people singing and bobbing and dancing in the grass and under the leaves all down below . . .

The name of the farm that was for sale was Hill Top. The sloping-roofed little farmhouse faced away from the village, looking over its own farm buildings to a rising pasture, scalloped at the far end with woods. It had a tangled garden of herbs, flowers, and vegetables. It had a rose vine climbing across the broken kitchen window; a beehive set in the wall; a dairy; a few cows, pigs, and sheep. Beatrix had enough money to buy it. She did.

Of course, she couldn't actually live there right away. In the first place, the house needed fixing up and repairing; second, her parents would have been scandalized at such a thought. So she let a tenant run the farm for her, but she visited whenever she could.

After Norman's death she turned to Hill Top Farm for comfort. The gray English winters had to be lived through at Number Two, but when the daffodil buds were beginning to show slits of yellow, Beatrix usually managed to get away for a visit to Sawrey. And now that her parents spent almost every summer somewhere in the Lake District, it was easy to slip off for frequent visits to Hill Top.

There were so many things to do! Once she brought her friend Miss Woodward to go over the house with her, and they had a delightful time exploring. "There is one wall four feet thick, with a stair case inside it," she wrote. "I never saw such a place for hide and seek, and funny cupboards and closets." The main trouble was the rats; they had all sorts of hiding places in the walls and under the floors. It took a long time to get rid of them, even with the help of four or five cats.

It was three years before the house was finished and ready to live in. Beatrix had added a small wing to the house for her tenant farmer and his family, keeping the main house for herself. She also built on a large room, known as the "library," where she hung some of Bertram's paintings. She furnished the house with sturdy pieces of old-fashioned furniture—the kind she had seen in many country cottages. "I have got a pretty dresser with plates on it," she wrote to Millie Warne, "and some old-fashioned chairs; and a warming pan that belonged to my grandmother, and Mr. Warne's bellows. . . . I have not meddled with the fireplace. I don't dislike it. Besides, it might be wanted for another book *if* I should ever get around to doing one."

Already she had used Hill Top House as the set-

ting for three new stories—*The Tale of Tom Kitten*, *The Tale of Jemima Puddleduck*, and *The Roly-Poly Pudding*. The first two show the garden and the farm-yard; *The Roly-Poly Pudding* has fascinating glimpses of the kitchen with its huge fireplace and chimney, which Tom Kitten rashly tried to explore. With a chuckle, Beatrix had put herself into this story too. At the very end she wrote: "And when I was going to the post late in the afternoon—I looked up the lane from the corner, and I saw Mr. Samuel Whiskers and his wife on the run, with big bundles on a little wheel-barrow, which looked very like mine. . . . I am sure *I* never gave her leave to borrow my wheel-barrow!"

Forty-one years old.

Forty-two.

Forty-three.

The passing years didn't bother Beatrix a bit. She felt that now she was wading in actual down-to-earth life, and she adored it. The instincts of her Crompton farming ancestors suddenly came to life; she felt happier at Hill Top Farm, more at home, than she ever had in London. Mr. Cannon, her tenant farmer, was teaching Beatrix both to be a good farmer and also an expert sheepwoman. She was an excellent pupil. She was learning to be shrewd, even a little autocratic. Soon no one could fool her about lambs, crops, or the village activities. Even though she could only be at the farm for brief periods, she became very much a part of the community. In one letter she commented: "There are several rows going on. I am not in on them at present, but I think I shall soon be attacking the city council about manure. I am entitled by law to all the sweepings along my piece of property, but the city is using it to fill up holes."

She was also learning to be tough about slaughtering lambs and calves—a necessary part of farm life—and wringing the necks of geese, ducks, and chickens. It was hard sometimes, but she knew it must be done.

Mr. and Mrs. Potter would have been troubled and horrified had they known that Beatrix, increasingly well-to-do with money earned by her books, was buying more and more property—here a field, there a field, two more small farms, several whitewashed cottages, even a stone quarry. In the course of time she came to own literally half the village of Sawrey. But she continued to endure her winters far away in the house in Bolton Gardens. When it snowed in London, she fretted about her sheep out on the hills.

However, she did have a number of things that kept her busy through the winter. There were translations of her books to discuss. She gave up on the Welsh and Spanish versions, but she did concern herself with the French and German. She thought with glee how bemused and astonished her old governess Mademoiselle Meringue would have been over the bunnies Flotsaunt, Trotsaunt, Queue-de-Coton, and Pierre in

Pierre Lapin. Would she ever see the book, or realize that its author had once been her pupil?

The popularity of her books brought other problems, too. Without permission from Warnes', a German firm was making and selling "Peter Rabbit" dolls, and later a "Squirrel Nutkin" doll. Then an English lady wrote to ask if she might make Peter Rabbit wallpaper for nurseries.

There were letters to be answered, objections to be filed, efforts to get her books copyrighted in other countries so foreign publishers could not print them. Publishers in the United States were then in the habit of "pirating" books by foreign authors—printing them without permission and without paying for them. This had already happened to *Peter Rabbit.*

All these chores were in themselves interesting, and they greatly enlarged Beatrix's circle of friends and acquaintances. But it was at Hill Top that she found her greatest satisfaction and happiness. During the first eight years she spent there, she wrote and illustrated thirteen books, and many of these were about her house or farm or the village of Sawrey. In the early ones—like *The Tale of Tom Kitten, The Roly-Poly Pudding* or *Jemima Puddleduck*—it was the interior of her own house and the garden around it that she sketched. Later, as in *Ginger and Pickles*, she moved into the village itself and drew the little shops, the cottages and gardens. Still other books, such as

The Tale of Mr. Tod and *The Tale of Pigling Bland,* show bits of the hills and vales surrounding Sawrey.

Some villages vied with each other to have their houses or animals portrayed in her stories. "I have been entreated to draw a cat aged twenty 'with no teeth,' " she wrote to a friend. "The owner seemed to think the 'no teeth' was a curiosity and attraction; I should think the poor old thing must be rather worn out."

The villagers now accepted Beatrix as one of themselves. After all, did she not hoe her own turnips, get in her own hay? Didn't she dress as they did, with her heavy wool skirts, clogs on her feet, a sack or shawl about her shoulders in wet weather? All this was to Beatrix much dearer than praise of her books. She hated what she considered insincere attempts to compare her little paintings with those of the great English artists. She loved it when she was recognized as being knowledgeable about sheep.

And so Sawrey became more and more her home. Mr. and Mrs. Potter did nothing to hinder her frequent visits to Hill Top, although she could sense their reluctance and disapproval. Perhaps they believed that a certain amount of freedom would make her more satisfied, less likely to become "queer" and "eccentric" in the Crompton fashion.

But now Beatrix began to dream of escaping from Bolton Gardens altogether and making a new life for herself, as Bertram had done.

A Wonderful Decision

GRADUALLY A new and unexpected complication came into Beatrix's life.

Four years after she had bought Hill Top Farm, full of her dream that she would stay at Sawrey, she bought Castle Farm, whose fields joined the fields of Hill Top. The house was pleasant, in excellent condition, and somewhat larger than Hill Top, which by now was pretty crowded with Beatrix, the Cannon family, and Beatrix's always growing collection of pets.

It was a Mr. William Heelis who drew up the contract for the sale of Castle Farm. Mr. Heelis was a country solicitor who had lived all his life in the Lake District. He had helped Beatrix with many of her other land purchases, and they had become good friends. She found herself turning more and more to this tall, quiet, understanding man for help and advice. Almost to her dismay, she discovered eventually that this friendship was developing into something stronger and warmer on both sides. For William Heelis wanted to marry her, and Beatrix could not decide what she should do.

On the one hand, she longed for the peace and security marriage would bring. A life at Sawrey with William Heelis would be her dream of happiness fulfilled. But on the other hand, could she distress her now ageing parents again? Could she face the reproaches, the arguments, the bitter words that were sure to be spoken?

In her distress of mind, she fell ill with influenza, which left her weak and depressed and in no state of health to face a family upheaval. Nevertheless she felt she had to tell her parents, and the result was just what she had expected; they would not hear of such a proposal. Who was this Mr. Heelis anyway? A mere country solicitor! This was what had come of her trying to live an independent life!

Rather to her surprise, Bertram came to her defense, traveling down from Scotland to give his support and to tell his parents he had long ago married without their permission and was perfectly happy with the farmer's daughter who was his wife.

Under the strain of family friction, Beatrix's health broke down completely. "I have been resting on my back for a week," she wrote to Harold Warne, who had been urging her to take care of some business matters. "My heart has been rather disturbed, but I am assured it will recover with quiet."

But she had no quiet at Bolton Gardens, where she had to listen daily to her parents' reproaches. It was her doctor who finally made it possible for her to escape, by advising her to leave the city for a while.

"Have you any special place you'd like to go so early in the spring?" he asked—rather slyly, Beatrix suspected; for Hill Top Farm was becoming increasingly famous, and Dr. Middleton had been rather impressed to find his patient was a celebrity.

"Well, yes," said Beatrix. "I do have a place. A farm at Sawrey."

"Perhaps leaving London and resting there would help you."

"My parents would object. Sometimes they let me get away early in the spring, although not quite as early as this. But now I'm ill . . . And besides. . . ."

"Besides what?"

"I might want to stay."

"And not come back to London at all?" This really astounded Dr. Middleton.

"I know what you're thinking," said Beatrix unhappily. "My parents are old and growing older. I ought not to leave them."

"But, for the most part, you have always respected their wishes."

"For the most part, yes." Beatrix sighed.

Dr. Middleton said, "Well, then, let me be frank with you. Your heart is not strong. Right now, worrying about others is hardly the best medicine for you."

Dejectedly Beatrix said, "Yes, I know."

"Go to your farm," said Dr. Middleton. "That is, if there is someone there to take care of you?"

"Oh, yes, Mr. and Mrs. Cannon."

Dr. Middleton got to his feet and stood staring down at his patient, obviously wanting to ask another question. Instead, he told Beatrix he would go and talk to her parents. Then, in spite of himself, out came the question.

"Are you doing another book, Miss Potter?"

"I've started one, but I don't know that I shall finish it."

"Oh, but you must! I'm sure you know some of your pictures have been compared to those of the great English masters."

"Rubbish!" interrupted Beatrix strongly. "I mean rubbish that they're so compared. I'm not getting excited nor do I mean to sound rude, Dr. Middleton, but it makes me impatient when people think I'm anything but what I am—the writer and illustrator of a number of books that amused me. Doing them amused me because one of the loves of my life has always been animals. Children and gardens, too. That's all. . . . Well, good luck in your talk with my parents. I'm sure you'll succeed, and I promise to write you from Hill Top."

The change did help, and three weeks later Beatrix wrote to Harold Warne: "I seem to get well slowly. I am stronger, but I was completely stopped by a short hill as I was trying to walk to the next village this afternoon and had to turn back. Nevertheless, I'm fairly sure I'm best out of London."

Perhaps Beatrix was. But just as Hill Top had always been on her mind in London, so Mr. and Mrs. Potter were constantly with her at the farm. In fact, it seemed as though nothing could lift her out of a very deep depression. Even when Mrs. Cannon, while rummaging around for something Beatrix wanted, found parts of her childish journal, Beatrix, though diverted, was not cheered. She happened to read an entry about one of her grandmother's admirers who had drowned himself, for love of her, in a lily pond. "It was all dreadfully sad," Beatrix's grandmother had reported calmly, "when you come to think of it."

When you come to think of it! Hadn't pretty Jessie Crompton cared more for this young man than that?

But this discovery was only a passing distraction, lasting no more than a few minutes. It would not have lasted that long if Beatrix had not had to struggle with the code writing she had invented all those years ago.

"Put it away," she told Mrs. Cannon wearily. And to herself she thought, Why do I keep those old journals? No one has ever read them—I suppose no one ever will. They'd have to learn my code first, and I've never told anyone about it.

Then back she settled into feelings of guilt and worry. She kept more and more to her house, going out only at night, refusing to be visited by the kind and concerned village people.

But one morning she felt she could not bear the confinement of staying in the house any longer. She must get out or she would suffocate! She decided to walk to the top of Oatmeal Crag and rest there. It would be quiet and peaceful, with just the sky above. Then she could think things through and decide what she should do.

Hurriedly she dressed, yet for some reason taking extra care with her appearance. It was a cool day, so she wore two flannel petticoats, a long tweed skirt and a matching coat with three buttons which, although buttoned all the way up, still did not conceal the pretty lace collar of her blouse. Last of all she pulled on a pair of extra heavy boots, the kind she and Mr.

Cannon wore when they were rounding up sheep together.

Beatrix left the house. Slowly she walked toward Oatmeal Crag. Slowly she began to climb. Her heart began to pound, but she set her teeth and walked on. She hadn't gone far when she heard a voice.

"Beatrix!"

She refused to hear. She wanted to get away from everyone.

"Beatrix Potter. Stop. Wait for me." It was William Heelis, panting along behind her.

She turned her head. "No."

Mr. Heelis cupped his hands around his mouth so she could hear him better.

"Obey me," he shouted.

Beatrix didn't exactly obey, but suddenly her legs wouldn't work. William Heelis caught up with her, his face red with exertion, twisted with worry.

"Are you trying to kill yourself?" he asked in a voice very different from his usual one.

Kill myself! The words shocked Beatrix out of her trancelike state. She wouldn't do that, no matter how she felt.

"Of course not," she retorted sharply. "I just wanted to get up into the hills and think. . . . Oh, William, my head has been going round and round from thinking. I don't want to be a sadness to my parents or a problem to you. I told you how it was when I had planned to marry Norman Warne. My parents objected because he was a publisher; they object to you because you buy and sell real estate. I'm not up to much of anything these days. I just don't see how I can wage this kind of battle again. Really I don't, William dear."

William Heelis took her hand, drew her down beside him on a sun-warmed rock. "Not up to being the best sheepwoman in the Lake District? Not up to being a famous author—now, all right, all right, I know how you feel about that—not up to being the shrewdest land buyer in all England? And, Madam, does not that put you in the real estate business too? What's more, have you forgotten that you promised to be my wife? And are you not an honorable woman?"

Beatrix pulled her hand away and laughed, somewhat shakily.

"Oh, William, you are such a comfort. I've been so worried—you can't imagine."

"My dear, you must let me share your worries now. A trouble shared is halved, you know."

They sat together, quietly, for a long time, looking out over the valley. Beatrix seemed to soak in peace and comfort from the warm sunshine. At last William pulled her to her feet and slowly, arm in arm, they walked back to Hill Top together.

That evening William told Beatrix that sometimes there came a time when a child had to become a parent to his parents. A time when the child had to make the decisions.

"Oh, William, you don't know them!"

"I shall, very soon."

William Heelis lost no time in taking charge. He summoned Bertram from Scotland and went with him and his wife to call on Mr. and Mrs. Potter. William had forbidden Beatrix to make the tiring trip to London herself, but he gave her a full report of what occurred. Bertram's wife, he said, rosy and plump and looking like the farmer's daughter she was, had been very sweet—yes, and motherly—to the bewildered Potters; what's more, they had seemed to appreciate this, and even to like her.

As for the rest, faced with William's tactful firmness, the Potters' objections to his marriage with Beatrix became feebler and feebler. They were persuaded that the great step should be taken, and soon. But first Beatrix wrote to Millie Warne: "I who have always confided in you have felt uncomfortable and guilty for some time, especially when you asked about Sawrey . . ." She ended the letter by saying: "I truly do not believe Norman would object."

As soon as Castle Farm was readied for them, the newly wed Mr. and Mrs. Heelis moved in. "Dear

Millie," Beatrix wrote only a week after their marriage, "by a friend I am sending a belated cake which I hadn't the courage to do before. This is to show you what a good cook I've become. My heart has completely recovered. I am very happy. Sincerely, Beatrix Potter Heelis, but whatever the name, always your loving sister. Come see us soon."

Millie Warne did. She visited often and Beatrix kept up her affectionate friendship with the Warnes.

Beatrix and William had a truly golden span of years together, delighted with their several farms, their sheep, their work in the garden, their putterings in the kitchen, icehouse, smokehouse. They remained two cheerful and zestful old people who loved and cherished each other.

What Happened Later

BEATRIX ENJOYED A LONG and happy life with William Heelis at Castle Farm. She could now forget completely the closed-in days at Number Two Bolton Gardens—"my unloved childhood home," as she had called it—in the freedom and loving companionship of her new life.

Country life suited her perfectly. She became a respected member of the Herwick Sheep Breeders Association and attended all the sheep fairs in the district, sometimes as an exhibitor, sometimes as a judge. In her shapeless tweeds she made an odd figure, but she cared little for that. A true Crompton now, she paid little attention to conventions. She loved walking in the hills and watching the animals there, sometimes sitting motionless for hours on end amid the rocks and heather.

Mr. Potter died only a few months after Beatrix's marriage, and her mother then gave up the house at Number Two Bolton Gardens and went to live in one of the houses near Lake Windermere that they had sometimes rented for summer vacations. Here she kept up the same life of careful routine she had always known—sewing, writing letters, going out for drives, making calls. Beatrix hoped that she was happy.

Busy as she was with her farm work, Beatrix had little time for writing or painting. It was not until five years after her marriage that she brought out a new book—*The Tale of Johnny Town Mouse*—the first "Tale" since *The Tale of Pigling Bland*. After this there were only a very few, spread out over a period of fifteen years—*The Fairy Caravan, The Tale of Little Pig Robinson, Sister Anne*—together with some books of nursery rhymes. Her eyes now were not equal to doing the fine, detailed work of her earlier books, even if she had wanted to.

But though she was writing no new books, her old ones were becoming more and more famous. The children of England and then of America and Europe took them to their hearts. To her amazement, Beatrix found that these little tales which she had done mainly for her own amusement or to please her young friends were being seriously acclaimed as "nursery classics."

Scores of imitators sprang up, but none could rival the originals.

Shy of all this praise, Beatrix tried to hide herself at Sawrey under the name of Mrs. Heelis. She resented the "trippers" who came to Sawrey to stare at her over the garden wall, but when visitors came all the way from America to talk about her books, she felt sincerely honored. "I always tell nice Americans to send other nice Americans along," she wrote to one of them. "You come because you understand the books and love the same old tales that I do—not from any impertinent curiosity."

As the years went on, she bought up more and more bits of property around the Lake District—nearly 3,000 acres in all. This was not for herself, but to save areas of natural beauty from being spoiled or destroyed by greedy real estate developers. Remembering Canon Rawnsley and his passion for saving beauty spots, she turned this property over to the National Trust for protection. Much of the money she made from the sale of her books went for this purpose.

These last years of her life were perhaps the happiest. Even the outbreak of World War II in 1939 could not upset her serenity, though it meant more hard work on the farm. But she was growing old now, and the cold, hard winters at Sawrey caused her health to fail. At last, on December 22, 1943, she died, peacefully and quietly, as she lay looking out her window at the nearby hills.

Strangely, much of the journal Beatrix wrote in her secret code, and which she had thought no one would ever read but herself, came to light again some twenty years after her death. A bundle of papers and exercise books filled with tiny writing was found at Castle Farm. At first no one could imagine what it was, but after several years of patient work the secret of the code was finally discovered and the journal could be read. It was found to be a remarkable record of Beatrix Potter's thoughts and activities during a most interesting part of her life—the growing-up years of fifteen to thirty.

One passage toward the end of her journal expresses the feeling that went into the making of her books, and helps to explain the secret of their magic for children:

> *I remember I used to half believe and wholly play with fairies when I was a child. What heaven can be more real than to retain the spirit-world of childhood. . . .*

A LIST OF BEATRIX POTTER'S BOOKS

1901   THE TALE OF PETER RABBIT (privately printed)

1902   THE TALE OF PETER RABBIT (Frederick Warne & Company, Inc.)

1902   THE TAILOR OF GLOUCESTER (privately printed)

1903   THE TAILOR OF GLOUCESTER (Frederick Warne & Company, Inc.)

1903   THE TALE OF SQUIRREL NUTKIN

1904   THE TALE OF BENJAMIN BUNNY

1904   THE TALE OF TWO BAD MICE

1905   THE TALE OF MRS. TIGGY-WINKLE

1905   THE PIE AND THE PATTY-PAN

1906   THE TALE OF JEREMY FISHER

1906   THE STORY OF THE FIERCE BAD RABBIT

1906   THE STORY OF MISS MOPPET

1907   THE TALE OF TOM KITTEN

1908   THE TALE OF JEMIMA PUDDLE-DUCK

1908   THE ROLY-POLY PUDDING

1909   THE TALE OF THE FLOPSY BUNNIES

1909   GINGER AND PICKLES

1910   THE TALE OF MRS. TITTLEMOUSE

1911   THE TALE OF TIMMY TIPTOES

1911   PETER RABBIT'S PAINTING BOOK

1912   THE TALE OF MR. TOD

1913   THE TALE OF PIGLING BLAND

1917   APPLEY DAPPLY'S NURSERY RHYMES

1918   THE TALE OF JOHNNY TOWN-MOUSE

1922   CECILY PARSLEY'S RHYMES

1925   JEMIMA PUDDLE-DUCK'S PAINTING BOOK

1929   PETER RABBIT'S ALMANAC

1929   THE FAIRY CARAVAN (privately printed)

1929   THE FAIRY CARAVAN (David McKay, Philadelphia)

1930   THE TALE OF LITTLE PIG ROBINSON (David McKay; Frederick Warne & Company, Inc.)

1932   SISTER ANNE (David McKay)

1944   WAG-BY WALL (Frederick Warne & Company, Inc.)

1956   THE TALE OF THE FAITHFUL DOVE (limited edition)

1956   THE TALE OF THE FAITHFUL DOVE (F. Warne & Co. Inc., New York)